ROOKIE TRUCK DRIVER

GARY H. BAKER

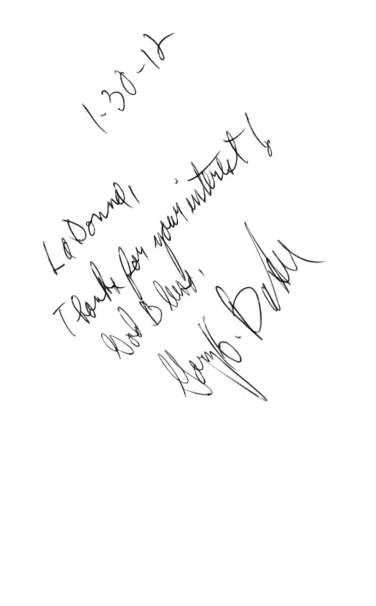

1-30-12

LaDonna!
Thank for your interest to
God Bless,
George Beverly

*This book is dedicated to
all truck drivers everywhere.*

A special thanks to my darling Debbie,
steadfast Nelda,
and miraculous Jan.

Chapter One

Toby Etheridge felt compelled to *do something*. On the morning of September 11, 2001 he had been on his way to work listening to his favorite country music station. When the news of the attack on the World Trade Center inundated all the radio air waves he turned his pick-up truck around and drove the six miles back to his home. He called his work, told them he'd be late and like most Americans, sat stunned in front of the TV watching the various news channels replay the towers collapsing over and over for an hour. But unlike most Americans, as he watched and listened to the various reporters scramble for information, he began making a mental list of the emergency supplies he would pick up on his way into work. Toby was accustomed to making quick assessments. It was, of course, too early to know if he and his family would be forced to actually use the supplies, but he didn't want to take any chances. Decision made, Toby was ready to act.

He was surprised to find that the local Wal-Mart and the nearby filling station weren't yet overrun with panic stricken shoppers. Only a few predictable verbal responses did he hear from the old men on the benches inside the store: "The 'Eye Rakkis' I reckon, is behind it. We should a gone into Baghdad back in '92 when we had the chance!"

"No, it wasn't the 'Eye Rakkis' neither. I'll bet it's a Tim McVeigh copycat."

Then, the always popular sentiment in Toby's hometown of Lake Thomas, Alabama, "It was the communist. Had to be. They been laying low all these years'til the time was right. Make no mistakes about it. It was the communist." Al-Qaeda was a word, a force, none of them had ever heard of before.

Toby wasted no time filling his shopping cart with flashlights, batteries, non-perishable food, bottled water, chain saw supplies, four 5-gallon gasoline containers, and then, his last stop on the way to the check-out, a 30/30 deer rifle, five boxes of cartridges, and five boxes of 12-gauge shotgun shells for the old 12-gauge he had at home.

By the end of that night he had made his first decision. If there were no further attacks during the early morning hours, the next day, he would pack up his truck and go to New York City to volunteer for whatever relief work they would put him in. If, on the other hand, more attacks came during the night or early morning hours, he would re-evaluate his plans. Sarah and the kids would have to be protected. As well intentioned as his desire was to help on the East Coast, to *do something*, his primary responsibilities were, of course, to stay in Lake Thomas to protect and take care of his wife, daughter, and son.

He thought back to his four years in the Navy during the war with Vietnam and the irony that during his twelve month tour of duty in the war zone, he or his ship was never shot at, was never under attack, but now, thirty-two years later, he couldn't guarantee that his small town of Lake Thomas, Alabama wasn't under attack at this very moment. It really got him fighting mad. Toby realized that he didn't handle things as well at forty-nine as he did thirty years ago. He could get angry very fast. He had been growing more aware of his short fuse for at least the last ten years. So far, he had not hurt anyone, but he acknowledged, if only to himself, that there was a dark side that threatened to emerge from the otherwise likeable man he was.

So, on the morning of September 12, 2001 Toby Etheridge was paying close attention to all the follow up news of the attacks on the Twin Towers, the Pentagon, and the plane crash in Pennsylvania, which would have been the third attack. Over the night and early into this new day he had built up an internal rage. His wife, Sarah, was concerned. Like Toby, she had been aware of his ever increasing short fuse, and last night at the dinner table, Toby's cursing and rage over the attacks had made it a very unpleasant evening for everyone.

Yesterday, after his stop for supplies, Toby had gone to the golf course. He had caught up on his list of things to do, and he had worked until dark. Most of what was needed to be done today was already out of the way, so Toby decided to take a full day off. More often than not, Toby was able to adjust his schedule just about any way he needed.

His boss, Billy Waynick, the club pro, was easy to get along with, now. Billy was aware that Toby knew things about him. Four years back the true nature of Billy Waynick had been revealed to Toby. Billy was a sexual sociopath. He had become careless and was caught red handed or rather bare-assed, by Toby on two occasions. After that Toby was able to pry open the entire smut box on Billy. The list included peep holes into the women's locker room, possession of child porn, a few in-the-woods encounters with gay members, and more than one sexual liaison with a prominent member's wife. It was then that Toby had laid out his ultimatum. He told Billy he would forgive and forget if Billy would promise to enter counseling and never again act out on his sexual predatory nature at the golf course. Billy agreed, and in the last four years, Toby had not seen or heard anything indicating Billy was back on the prowl. But, recognizing his nature, Toby had warned Billy, more than once, that if he ever had reason to suspect Billy of trying anything with his wife or kids, he would kill him. And Toby meant it. It was amazing that the two men could still work as closely as they did and not come to blows. Billy knew, that if Toby ever decided to disclose the dirt to the club owners, it *would* mean the end of his job and career. So, no, Billy had no desire to create problems for Toby.

This morning Toby was sitting at the kitchen table while Sarah was fiddling with toast and eggs at the counter. Listening to the TV news they were both relieved that no additional attacks had been reported. "I'll bet the airline pilots added a few extra gray hairs yesterday," Toby said. He was trying to be casual and make small talk so as to let Sarah know he was under control this morning, as opposed to last nights exhibition of rage. She knew better, as evidenced by his tossing and turning all night and the fact that he'd been up at four a.m. checking out his new rifle.

"Honey, you didn't sleep much, did you?" She never had solutions for his restlessness of late, but she felt like it was at least something of a comfort to him to let him know that she was aware of it and that she knew it would mean a difficult day ahead.

"No, not too much." Then he realized now was as good a time as any to tell her about his plans, about his first decision.

"Sarah, I've got to go to New York."

She was prepared for it. She knew by the tone of his voice there would be no use in opposing him.

"Well honey, how do you think you can help them? I know you want to be there, but what do you think you could do?"

He knew she was trying to be supportive, and he loved her too much to be less than candid. "You know, I'm not really sure. I just know I've got to do something. I called the Marine recruiters yesterday. They won't take me. I'm too old."

"The Marines! Toby tell me you didn't try to enlist in the Marines. I can't believe you would do that. You didn't even tell me?"

Her patience with him had its limits. "Toby what would you do in the Marines at your age?"

"I told you, they won't take me. But by God if they would, I'd try to kill as many terrorists as I possibly could. That's what I'd do!"

Sarah didn't doubt that he would have tried to kill terrorists. She wanted to sit down and talk this through with him. She knew how tenacious he could be once he got an idea in his head, but she was nearly late to work. Any further discussion would have to wait until tonight. She pecked him on his forehead with a quick kiss and off to work she went, leaving him with his coffee and added teasingly, "Honey, I love you, but please promise me you won't try to join the Army today."

After Sarah left Toby poured himself another cup of coffee and sat at their kitchen table. He continued to listen to the news and mulled over his options. He was very disappointed, even a little angry that his second decision had been thwarted. He always knew that if the opportunity ever came that his country needed him again, that he would do it. And that if that time came, he wanted in on the ground floor this time. He'd volunteer to be a grunt- to carry a weapon and look for bad guys.

Toby had carried something of a guilt complex with him ever since Vietnam. He knew vets his own age that were scarred for life, and of course he knew some that never came home. He'd had an internal dialogue with these guys for twenty-eight years. *You paid the price. I should have. I promise you I will do the dirty work the next time. All you guys at Khe Sahn, Hue, the highlands, you on the rat patrols, you on the swift boats, you in the Mekong Delta, you at Lang Vei, the Ia Drang Valley, and all the rest of you. I'll see you in heaven, or I'll see you in hell, but I will see you, and when I do, I too will have paid some or all of the same price you paid.*

Chapter Two

Toby's day off did not go as he had planned. He had planned to get his preparations made so that he would have his home affairs buttoned down and be able to leave that night to go to New York to help with the rescue effort. However, all morning reporters had been announcing that the authorities in New York and Washington were urging Americans not to come to the East Coast to help unless they were part of a specific group or organization that was solicited to do so. Already, there were problems with non-emergency personnel getting in the way of rescue and relief work. Since Toby was mostly a loner, he was not affiliated with any of those groups. So, he spent most of the morning making calls to friends, the local police, fire and rescue groups, town and county government offices, and local service organizations. He hit a stone wall. Those he made contact with told him that they were not going North and had not yet formulated any local emergency plans. They were waiting for the Feds to notify them if there was any necessity to do so. They would let him know, but right now they did not need any help but thanked him for his concern. About the tenth call, Toby slammed the phone down impatiently. "Wait," he sputtered. "Wait for what? All Hell to break loose?" Well, he could still get things ready for himself and his family to be protected. So he took his new 30/30 back by the tree line on the edge of his meager ten acre farm to shoot at some bottles and cans he lined up at one-hundred paces. He might as well get familiar with this rifle. He might have to use it.

Ronnie Matlock heard him back there and urged his old rusty pick-up truck up the hill and through the brush.

"Coon Dog you old rattlesnake, I thought you'd be fishing today," Toby said.

Coon Dog loved it when an opportunity like this came along, and these opportunities came along on a regular schedule – nearly every time he'd go fishing. "Done been fishing," he said in his slow, deadpan, country best. Then he slowly opened the lid on the big ice cooler in the truck bed for Toby's inspection of eight frying pan sized stripers and three huge smallmouth bass, one of which was a good foot and a half long and probably went seven pounds.

"It doesn't look like you left any fish for the rest of the county." Toby primed, already knowing what Coon Dog's response would be.

"I left plenty of fish. It's just that the rest of the county don't know where to find them." Coon Dog closed the lid on the cooler. Most people in and around Lake Thomas didn't use Ronnie's old family nickname of Coon Dog. Many of them didn't know it, and those that did were reluctant to use it because Ronnie would snap at them if the exact intonation was not used when calling him Coon Dog. Ronnie's daddy, Horace Matlock, had a unique way he pronounced the nickname –'C-O-O-O-O-ON Doggy,' and if you didn't say it to Ronnie just like Horace said it, well, you'd be better off not saying it at all. Now and then you'd hear about Ronnie hitting someone who didn't pronounce the nickname correctly. It was a way he honored his Daddy's memory.

"I heard you popping off a few rounds. What are ya' shooting at?"

"Just trying to sight this new gun in."

Coon Dog was eyeing the rifle. Toby handed it to him. Coon Dog expertly worked the action several times and loaded it with three rounds. He then got an old empty cardboard oil can box from his truck, walked out to where the cans and bottles were scattered, and placed a can on a rock on the ground so that it was dead center in the middle of the cardboard box behind it. He walked back to Toby, then to his truck and found a hatchet which he took to the edge of the woods and hacked off three skinny saplings. He notched the saplings and fastened them with a string and then spread the legs below for the tripod. He rested the barrel of the rifle in the top of the tripod, took four seconds to aim, released the safety, took another three seconds for a calming breathe, then squeezed off a shot. The can didn't move.

"I'll bet it's high right." Coon Dog walked back to the box and found the entry hole in the cardboard a half inch high right of the can. Next, he made adjustments on the scope, squeezed off another round, repeated the process one more time, and on his last return from the cardboard box he handed Toby a tin can with one perfectly dead center clean hole in it on one side, and a jagged torn out larger hole on the other side.

"She's good at a hundred yards. You'll need to allow about two inches though if you get a stout cross wind. What are you going to kill? You're not a deer hunter."

"Yeah, well, you know, I thought maybe I might have to become a deer hunter. I think it's possible there will be food shortages. Hey, if those filthy ragheads take out our computers and communications, we're going to be in a world of trouble, and don't count out poisoning our food and water supply. I don't think we've seen anything yet."

Coon Dog allowed that he had to agree with Toby. The only difference was that Coon Dog already was living off the land for the most part. The 9-11 attacks and the possibility of more devastating attacks on the U.S. economy, infrastructure, and food supplies were not going to force him into a survivalist lifestyle. He was nearly in that mode now, of his own volition. If he needed to go just a little beyond what he was already doing, it wouldn't be difficult for Coon Dog.

Later that night, September 12, 2001, Toby sat in the clearing near the woods about two hundred yards from his house. He had a shed up there for his tractor and tools, and he had made a roughed-out shelter for camping out, or sitting by the campfire which he did a lot of, usually alone, but sometimes with Sarah, Derrick or Carolyn. This was his place, his comfort zone, his thinking and contemplative place – his spiritual place. Here he could pray.

Toby's praying had always produced results. Just like his preacher exclaimed from the pulpit, "When we earnestly pray for God's intervention, for His blessings, for a sign from our Heavenly Father, we *will* have our prayers answered. They may not be the answers we want, but we *will* get answered prayer." And, so it was with Toby. He had to admit that the Lord most times answered his prayers in a positive manner, as evidenced by the first panic attack he had a few years back. He and several other parents had chaperoned a group of students including his son, Derrick, on a European summer trip. Just about anything that could go wrong, did go wrong.

Toby used to pride himself on his ability to stay fresh, alert and mentally keen in pressure situations, but on this trip he found himself barely hanging on. The students of course tested him and the other parents at every opportunity. Then their reservations had been mishandled in Zurich, and they were lucky to find a youth hostel that grudgingly accepted them for two nights. Several students came down with a virus of some sort which had threatened to send the entire group back home early. It was one thing after another. And finally, after they all arrived back home in Alabama, one of the younger boys, fourteen, realized his parents could not pick him up at the airport because they had been called away to California on an emergency business trip. The boys aunt, could take him, but she lived over two hundred miles away in Mobile. It was the only place he could go. Needless to say, Toby got the call to drive the boy to his aunt's home.

The trip down from the Birmingham airport was uneventful, but during the drive back towards Lake Thomas the last piece of mortar in the brick wall that had formerly been Toby's mental fortitude, crumbled. Toby experienced a full blown, classic, panic attack. He had not slept in nearly three days, and when finally the stress, frustration and fatigue of the last two weeks settled in on him on his drive back to Lake Thomas, the implosion overwhelmed him. Derrick was with him when it happened, but Toby tried not to let him know what was happening. Derrick didn't understand why his Dad wanted to stop and eat and relax for an hour, since they were only two hours from home. He knew it wasn't like his Dad to waste time traveling when they were that close to home, but Toby had no choice. He had to stop! Driving became impossible. He felt as though an immense six foot thick, solid steel curtain was closing in on him from all directions.

He had never experienced anything like this before. He had never paid any attention to "the walls closing in on you" reports that panic attack victims often described. The actual physical feeling that he was being crushed was not all of it. He also felt as if he no longer had control – of anything. He was certain that if he continued driving he would be the cause of an accident. He sensed he might harm someone if he continued. He was uncertain of everything else. Why was this happening? What had caused it? Would he die? He certainly felt like it. Toby managed to reach the next interstate exit and pull in to a restaurant parking lot. He lied to Derrick, "I'm hungry, let's stop a while."

Toby felt a little better after ordering a meal and starting on a cup of coffee, but still the vice was closing in on him. If he didn't get some fresh air soon, he was going to…, he didn't know what. But it wasn't good. He told Derrick he would be right back. He walked outside and started jogging across a field. He was heading to a wooded thicket nearly three hundred yards away. When he got far enough away to be out of sight, he stopped and sobbed. Doing the only thing he could think of, he threw his arms skyward and begged God to help him, to save him.

At that moment Toby was sure he could not continue. Driving himself and his son home was out of the question. He felt he might even have to call paramedics to come get him and take him to the nearest hospital. Again he threw his eyes to the sky and plead, "Father, I don't know what is happening to me. Help me, please. If it is Your will for me to stop here and go to a hospital, then so be it. I'm in your hands." With that Toby brought his arms and eyes down from the sky and slowly walked back to Derrick and the restaurant. Toby had been attending a small church near his home mostly as a concession to his wife. He had always felt that church was a place for woman and children. He felt he could be close to God anywhere and really didn't need the church thing. But recently they had gotten a new Pastor who spoke in a way that said some things that Toby had been moved to consider. He had heard the Pastor say that challenges get worse because we don't ask God to help us with them. That thought had stuck with him, and he had started asking and praying more often. That day he latched on to that response as a lifeline.

Things got better. The horrendous vice that had been closing in around him eased off, and the total feeling of helplessness and impending disaster began to dissolve. The talisman of prayer had saved him. He was able to drive himself and Derrick home safely. There was no hospital mental ward that day.

Tonight, thinking, watching the campfire, Toby realized he would have to ditch both his first decision that the 9–11 attacks had generated, the decision to go to New York to help in the rescue and relief work, and his second decision that the Marines had dashed because of his age.

He decided to talk with God. "Father, I'm hurting big time. I need to be doing something for my country, but I'm confused. I understand you not wanting me to go to New York to help. I just don't know what you want me to do. There's got to be something. Believe me, Father, I'll do it if you just show me what it is." As he thought and prayed, a brilliantly streaking falling star caught his attention. Then, only a few moments later, a second meteor as brilliant as the first, burned into the night sky on a similar trajectory. Three seconds later, like the first one, it too, vanished. Toby's alertness spiked. Now he felt an answer was in the offing. What was the final sign going to be? What action was God going to direct Toby to take? Another twenty minutes went by. Toby had intensified his praying and questioning. "God, what is it You want me to do?" The third falling star flashed quickly in the same area and on the same trajectory as the first two. Toby immediately understood the incredible spiritual experience he was feeling and witnessing. Three falling stars – the Trinity.

This wasn't the first time God had yanked Toby's errant mental capacities back into focus with a visceral and visual sign from the night sky. Sarah was the only other human that knew about these visions, signs, events, that Toby had been experiencing for years. She wasn't as sure about the authenticity of their origin as Toby was. On the other hand, she didn't doubt the fact that Toby was always totally convinced of their origin and purpose – God was giving him a direct sign, a vision of His will.

It was no different tonight. Toby's spirit interpreted the three meteors as the unmistakable presence of God. The certainty of this fact Toby felt in the very marrow of his bones. Also, finally, at the instant he witnessed the third meteor, Toby received insight to God's answer. God wanted him to become a big rig truck driver. At first Toby questioned this directive, but as he slowly thought it through, he realized, just like other times in the past, he didn't *have to* understand it. Yes, he had been thinking about quitting his job as the head groundskeeper at the golf course for some time now. And, he had been considering starting a new career as an over-the-road truck driver. What confused him about the sign God had just given him, was that he didn't see how driving a truck related in any way to his unyielding urge to physically and practically do something to respond in some way to the cold blooded attacks those Arab animals had so successfully launched against his country. He reminded himself that there must be a connection that God had in mind. Surely, with time, he would realize what it was. The more Toby thought about it, the more sense it made. God must have a job for him to do, something important, that could only be done while driving a big truck.

Toby's instincts were to act deliberately on whatever new direction God had aimed him. He would check it out; let it settle in; see how it felt for a few days. Then, if he was sure about it, he would run with it. But already, this new direction in Toby's life was taking control. As he walked down the hill towards the house he could see the lights on in the kitchen. Sarah would be there, preparing his lunch that he'd take to work with him tomorrow. How was he going to tell her she would soon be the wife of an over-the-road long distance truck driver?

This was his third decision after the events of 9-11 and he had a sense of the rightness of it. On the open road he could think, watch and wait for the opportunity he knew God had in mind for him. The shadow of a fourth idea, a reason why God might need a truck driver, was rumbling around deep inside the fringe of Toby's mind, fermenting, bubbling, waiting. He would not know whether it was another of God's directives he needed to act on, or if it was some inclination of evil. The truth of the matter was it was a little of both, and it just might trigger events that could easily spiral out of control. But for now, Toby knew what to do next and that was enough.

Chapter Three

Carolyn Etheridge, Toby's sixteen year old daughter, a sophomore class homecoming court attendant and rising star on the golf team, was on the first tee waiting for Chelsea Barber so they could get their afternoon practice round started. Her Dad would often play with them, but today he was two counties away buying new shrubs and Dogwood trees earmarked for landscaping around the clubhouse.

Chelsea was often late, so after another fifteen minutes, Carolyn decided to play alone. She hit her tee shot 212 yards straight down the middle and was walking off the tee, her pull cart in tow. She noticed Mr. Waynick up near the clubhouse wave in her direction, so she waved back. She liked her Dad's boss. He had always been very friendly to her, and Carolyn thought he was cute. Carolyn knew he was single, and she had heard some stories that had made the gossip circles concerning his non-golfing activities around the club, but she had never believed them.

It was a slow day at the Lake Thomas Golf Club, probably no more than three groups on the course playing, and they were well into the back nine. Forty minutes later Carolyn was leaving the number four green. This green tucked way back into the woods was restful and quiet. She saw Mr. Waynick coming towards her on a golf cart and thought perhaps he would join her game.

"Hi Carolyn, where's Chelsea?" Waynick was eyeing Carolyn up and down, from the red ribbon tying off her beautiful long strawberry-blond hair into a ponytail, all the way down her shapely body to her tanned athletic legs. He casually looked around to see if anyone was in view.

"Oh, she didn't show up. I waited for her a while, but I guess something came up and she couldn't make it." She caught the hunger in his eyes, and instead of being embarrassed or uneasy, she was proud of the fact that older men often were caught eyeing her as Billy was now.

Billy was out of the cart walking closer to her, "Carolyn, I've been thinking about next summer and an opening we might have here at the club. Would you be interested in working here?"

"Sure, Mr. Waynick. What would I be doing?" This would be too perfect, Carolyn thought. Working here where Dad is, and working for this super cute Billy Waynick. Her smile lit up, and she didn't notice the look Billy was giving her so much as she was thinking of being around the golf course all summer long. *How groovy that would be!* Then she realized Billy was very close to her, too close. He was leaning in to her, smelling her, and for some reason, breathing hard. Uneasy, Carolyn stepped back away from him a few feet and asked him again, "What would I be doing Mr. Waynick?"

Billy, unable to stop the throb bolting through him, stammered, "Uh, yeah, yeah, I've got a job for you all right. I've got a really good job for you, honey. Let me show you. Let me show you." He reached for the zipper under his fly, and his swollen erection burst out.

Carolyn didn't run, at first. She was locked, transfixed in a moment of shock, then her animal instincts kicked in, and she ran towards the number five tee, eighty yards away. It was the wrong direction to run. It was going further away from the clubhouse, but she would have had to run through Billy if she had gone the other way.

Billy leered with satisfaction. He had planned his approach well. He took off after her, his sexual arousal increasing. He was now totally into the thrill of the chase, his purpose cemented, his goal to conquer, and he was gaining on her.

Ronnie 'Coon Dog' Matlock was in the woods near the number four green. It was not unusual for him to be scouting for the upcoming deer season as early as September. In fact, it would have been unusual if he had not been in the woods. He was either scouting deer trails, killing a squirrel or two or identifying hawk's nests. The farmers and landowners in this end of the county were well aware that Coon Dog took game out of season from time to time. Even the game warden was aware of this, but none of them cared much about it. Coon Dog's knowledge of the woods and the wildlife was almost legendary, so when any of them needed advice or help to combat a problem in the woods, Coon Dog was the man they would come to with maybe a question about Coyotes or where a good patch of Ginseng might be found. Once, the state police sought Coon Dog's aid in locating a missing person they had reason to believe had been murdered and buried in the woods. In less than two days Coon Dog had picked up the trail and located the body back six miles in the roughest and most remote area in the county. The skills Coon Dog possessed came naturally. His daddy, his daddy's daddy, and on down the line for untold generations, the Matlock clan had been hunters, fishers, frontiersmen, and in Coon Dog's case, a United States Navy Seal in Vietnam.

The day Billy Waynick attacked Carolyn Etheridge, Coon Dog had been scouting a certain ten point buck he was planning on taking when the season opened. When it came to trophy bucks, Coon Dog always played by the rules. This particular buck had been spotted near the golf course several times, so Coon Dog thought it wise to spend a few mornings and afternoons there in an attempt to determine the deer's travel patterns. By opening day, Coon Dog would thoroughly know the buck's movements.

Carolyn had let out only one good scream before Waynick tackled her, but it was enough for Coon Dog to hear. He was on the downward slope of a hill facing the golf course some two hundred yards away in the woods. He didn't recognize the voice as being Toby's daughter, but he'd heard enough human distress signals in his days to know that someone was in trouble. He ran amazingly well for a fifty something year old, even with the six foot hickory staff he always had with him in the woods.

By the time Coon Dog came out of the woods, Waynick had managed to knock Carolyn to the ground and to rip open her golf shirt. He was going for her shorts when Coon Dog caught him on the back of the head with a roundhouse swing of the hickory staff. Fortunately for Waynick, his shoulder had deflected a good deal of the blow; otherwise, he would have been a dead man. He fell off the girl, rolled a half roll, came to his knees and was about to get up. Coon Dog dropped the staff and dove on him before he could get to his feet. Instinctively, he went for Waynick's throat and was squeezing off the air. "You sorry animal. Killing you would be too easy. I'll leave that for Toby if he wants." He left Waynick choking and gagging and turned to Carolyn who was sitting up now.

She had a bruise on her face, but she was not bleeding. She was crying and shaking, but she told Coon Dog she was all right. Coon Dog lifted her in his arms and carried her to Waynick's cart. Then he fetched Carolyn's pull cart, put it on the back, and started toward the clubhouse. He looked over his shoulder and saw Waynick still on the ground, writhing in pain and now spitting up blood. After releasing his death grip on Billy's throat, Coon Dog had placed several heavy gut kicks into Waynick and one perfectly placed groin kick. Coon Dog had no doubt Waynick would still be there when he got back.

On the ride back to the clubhouse Carolyn convinced Coon Dog that she really was all right. Her shaking and crying had ceased. She told Coon Dog she heard what he said to Waynick about letting Toby kill him. "Please don't tell Daddy. You can't! He *would* kill him. Please Ronnie, please don't."

Coon Dog had to agree. Toby probably would kill Billy if he learned about the attempted rape. He got Carolyn to her car, went to the ice machine around the back of the snack bar, then went back and put an ice pack up against her bruised jawbone. "I think you are right, Carolyn. We better not let this get out, at least for a while. I'll take care of things here. You go on back home, and if your Mom sees your face, well, just make up something. Okay?"

Carolyn hugged and thanked her rescuer. "I'm so grateful you were here."

Coon Dog choked out a grunt. He watched her drive off, then jumped back in the golf cart and headed back to the number five tee area. He saw Billy Waynick right where he left him. He aimed the golf cart at full speed at the nearest tree to Billy, then jumped off at the last second. He went to

Waynick and got his car keys out of his pocket and told him to stay put, that he was coming back for him, and was going to take him to the hospital. All Billy could do was cough up blood and continue to moan. Next he went back to the clubhouse. This time he went in through the front and found Martha Jones who worked the cash register and snack stand. "Martha, Billy has had an accident out by number five tee. I was in the woods scouting a deer trail and heard the crash. When I got to him I could see that the brakes must have failed coming down the hill, and Billy must have hit the tree head on. He's not hurt all that bad, but I think I'll take him to the hospital just to make sure. I've got his car keys, and I'll drive out to number five and pick him up, then get him into the E room just to get him checked out."

"Well, okay, I guess that would be the thing to do. Is there anything I can do to help?" She was aware of Coon Dog's reputation in times of trouble, and she trusted his decision totally.

"No, I don't think so. Where's Toby?"

"He's in Wayne County buying supplies."

"Just let Toby know what happened when he gets back. Don't worry; everything will be fine."

Chapter Four

Toby's application to Mountaintop Transport for their ten week driver training program had been approved. He was anxious to get started. He wondered what it was really like living in a truck for weeks at a time, roaming the country from coast to coast. The idea of being a trucker nomad had intrigued him for years. He'd heard and read a little about open road trucking and the mystique attached to truckers. He guessed soon enough he would understand a thing or two about it. He thought often about how God would use him as a trucker, but at the moment he was only certain about this first step and that there was something else that he would be told to do when the timing was right. But first he had to complete the two week on-site training in Memphis and then co-drive with a trainer for an additional four weeks. Finally, he would be required to co-drive an additional four weeks with another rookie truck driver. Then, and only then, would he be assigned his own truck and be set free as a solo driver. It seemed like an arduous process, but Toby guessed it was all necessary if he was to carry out his plans.

The day Toby left Lake Thomas for Memphis, Coon Dog was driving him to the Greyhound Station. Coon Dog was lighting a hand rolled cigarette when Toby jumped on him, "When are you going to throw those coffin nails away?"

"I reckon the day I walk through the pearly gates."

That figures, Toby thought. *Why do I bother to ask him? And that open bottle between the seats, I know better than to badger him about that.*

"Now before I forget it and you start asking any more dumb questions, I've got something for you. Look in that box there on the floor. That book belongs to you."

Toby didn't know what Coon dog was referring to. He looked in the box. Digging through a couple of tools, a couple of quarts of motor oil, and an oil blackened rag, he pulled out of it a cheap, worn paperback novel. Toby noticed the cover had a picture of a big semi rig chugging across some far off, wide open spaces. "Thanks, Coon Dog, you shouldn't have."

"I didn't. A feller down in the Louisiana bayou gave that book to me two weeks ago. I was down there with an old Cajun buddy of mine. We were doing a little gator trapping for the state. Anyway, the last night the county ag. agent threw us a little bayou swamp party. He set it up right nice. They had a gumbo stirred up that'd make your balls whistle. There was fancy shrimp and crawdaddy kebobs, Cajun barbequed goat and best of all they had a barrel of some vintage Cajun swamp whiskey that rattled your teeth down to your tail bone. Now I ask you, have you EVER met an ag. agent that didn't have a ready supply of white lightning? Why I can guarantee you that...."

Toby had heard enough to know he had to bring Coon Dog back to the subject at hand. "Coon Dog, what about the book?"

"Oh, yeah, roger that, old friend. Let's see now. There was an old 'Festus' looking truck driver down there. You remember, Festus on Gunsmoke? I always liked the way he'd say, Ma-at-th-ew, you know, real slow."

"Coon Dog!" Toby wondered how much of that open bottle between the seats had disappeared already today.

"Okay, all right, all right. He gave me the book and said, 'Now, look here, partner. You can read this if you want to, but what I really want you to do is take it back to Alabama with you. You've got a friend there that I'd like you to give it to.' Hell, I was so drunk, none of it made any sense to me. He might of given me a name or something, I don't remember. I just figured the next day, you know, when I was sobered up a little, that because it had a picture of a truck on the cover that he meant for me to give it to you. I never even looked inside."

Toby opened the book and thumbed through a few pages. Nothing caught his eye. Then, as he flipped back towards the front of the book he noticed a hand written note on the inside of the cover:

Driver, Be safe out there, and be careful about the decisions you make.

That was all there was except a small child-like drawing of an eighteen wheeler with some little puffs of black diesel smoke rising above the twin pipes. Toby counted them. There were seven.

An hour later he was on his way to the Mountaintop Transport training facility in Memphis. The Greyhound bus he was on carried mostly blacks. There was one young white couple that looked as if they had tried to gather up all their possessions in plastic bags before abandoning their most recent trailer park. They were arguing over whether the young man would get away with lighting up a cigarette. A black lady across the row from them said, "Honey, they throw you off this here bus. You best not try smokin' no cigarette." Then all three of them continued the argument. The fifty something black lady might have been the young man's mother. She set right in on him as if she'd known him all her life.

None of these proceedings seemed to distract Toby from the trucker paperback novel Coon Dog had given him. He had never done much reading before. Sometimes he'd read magazine articles for work or newspapers, but he left the novels to Sarah or the kids. Now he was curious to find out if there was a message for him contained in this book. He began reading page one.

* * *

The eighteen wheeler pulled over to the shoulder and waited on the hitchhiker.

"Climb aboard. Where you headed?"

The hitchhiker nearly lost his balance on the two and four foot high safety steps. He tossed his bag in on the floor, climbed on up into the shotgun seat, and pulled the door closed behind him.

"California. How far are you going?"

The truck driver didn't hesitate, "Going to heaven!"

Neither of them said anything. The hitchhiker braced himself wondering if this was going to be another one of those whacked-out, right-wing, Christian drivers who would preach at him the whole ride?

A moment later the truck driver added, "Before I get there, I've got to get this load to Flagstaff."

The hitchhiker sighed, smiled and settled back in

the seat. "Yes indeed. I understand. It seems we are always either on a journey or between journeys doesn't it?"

"I never thought about it like that, but I guess you are right." The driver pulled the big truck back out on the highway and methodically worked his way through about fourteen gears until he attained highway speed again.

The hitchhiker continued, "It seems like it's always been that way with me. I often think I've got a handle on the direction I'm going, then all of a sudden a new thought, a new inspiration comes along, and off I go into a new direction. Don't get me wrong. I like my life. I like changes. But sometimes it just seems maybe I've missed a turn somewhere. Do you ever feel like that?"

"Sure," the truck driver said. "I've felt like that occasionally. The main thing that keeps me going is the work, *this* work. Driving this rig all over; that's what it's about for me. My daddy used to keep a scripture pinned up on the wall over his desk. It said *In all labor there is profit, but idle chatter leads only to poverty*. That's what I've tried to live. Work hard every day and things will work out." He was satisfied with the way he stated his philosophy of life, and then he focused his attention on driving. Neither spoke for several minutes. They were content to watch the vast West Texas prairie speed by. It was mighty big out there. Nothing except the random patch of scraggly Mesquite, a wobbly barbed wire fence line trailing off to the horizon, and a lonely tumble weed now and then.

Eventually the truck driver continued, "I remember picking up a fellow in Georgia a few years ago. We got to talking, you know, kind of like you and me are now. I noticed how small a man he was when I pulled over. Sure enough, it turned out he had been a jockey in his younger days. He rode in the Kentucky Derby years ago. He told me he had lived the hard work ethic. He started as a stable boy at a horse ranch in Oklahoma, worked his way up to warm-up rider, and finally he became a jockey. It didn't stop there. He became a trainer and an owner. He owned two huge horse farms in Ocala, Florida. Oh, man! He had it all. Said he was the king of the show in Lexington and Louisville when he was up there. Even in Nashville. He'd gotten to know a lot of country music high rollers, and when he was in Nashville, he owned it. He told me he was so proud of all his accomplishments and all the famous people that paraded him around as their friend. Naturally, I wondered what happened to it all. Here he was hitchhiking. So I asked him. He said two divorces took it all. Well, sir, I've thought about that a considerable amount, and I've come to a different conclusion. I think it was probably booze that started the downhill spiral and that, of course, led to the lost work ethic. The divorces and his current state of affairs were just the natural outcome. The day I picked him up all he had was a small overnight bag, a pouch of tobacco, and rolling papers."

"Interesting," the hitchhiker said. "But do you not account for the possibility that the jockey turned jet-set idol could legitimately have had true and deep love? When that love burned up in tragedy, it destroyed the man's soul."

"I don't know. Maybe true and deep love is over-rated, and hard work doesn't get enough playing time."

The hitchhiker asked the truck driver if smoking would bother him. The truck driver said, "No, go ahead." The hitchhiker smoked a cigarette and they both marveled at the flat prairie of west Texas.

Later that night the truck driver told the hitchhiker a story about himself when he was a young man. "I was married to a beautiful girl. We lived in the Shenandoah Valley of Virginia and had two young sons. I was a high school teacher in those days. One year during the summer break I helped another teacher move his household to up-state New York where he had taken a new job. I drove a rented straight truck the 400 miles north and helped unload it. When the work was done my teacher friend paid me a couple hundred dollars. Well, sir, I had a choice. I could have caught a Greyhound back to Virginia or, I could save the money and hitch hike back. Since my wife and I were struggling to make ends meet, I knew the extra money would come in handy. So I chose to hitchhike.

Six p.m. found me on the southbound entrance ramp to I-81. My overnight bag was at my feet and my thumb was stuck out proper. I remember it was mid June and that far north there was still plenty of chill in the air. I'd been hitch hiking since age fourteen so I stood straight up and looked right into the face of would be ride providers as they sped by. Like anything else, you know, there is an art to good hitch hiking. You have to know where to stand and how to stand. You must give a good appearance and look clean cut. Most importantly, you must look like you'll work for your ride, like you'd be willing to stand out there straight up with good body language for ten hours if necessary. The arm and thumb must be perky, sticking out at a sharp angle. You've got to look like you really want that ride. This gives the message that you've got someplace to go. Many derelicts, homeless, or just plain lazy bums will actually hitchhike sitting down or leaning against a sign post, or the worst of all, walking with their back to traffic.

Not me. I thought I was a master hitchhiker. Be that as it may, I was beginning to think I'd have no luck that night. It was seven-thirty p.m. I'd been at it an hour and a half and it was getting dark. The cars and trucks all had their lights on. I knew in five more minutes it would be pitch black, and then the chances of my catching a good ride would be slim to none. Just then I noticed a big cream colored Buick Riviera pull over and wait for me. I came up to the passenger side door, took a quick appraisal and jumped in. The driver was a forty something male, pleasant appearance, dressed well, and had a nondescript, midwest-southern dialect. Best of all he told me he was on his way to Atlanta, and he said he'd be staying on I-81 south all the way through Virginia. Too good to be true I thought. One ride all the way home to Harrisonburg. After a few minutes idle chitchat, like where both of us were from and where we were going, I started to realize that there was *something* about him that I just could not put my finger on. What was it, I wondered? In just a few minutes with him I sensed a unique trait, a special gift he possessed, but still, I wasn't sure what? He seemed friendly enough, and certainly not a threat of any kind. I was usually pretty good at screening out any kind of sexual predator implications or psycho possibilities. No, this man had some character trait or talent that was not anti-social, but at the same time was very unusual. I wondered what was it about this man?

So I said to him, 'Thanks for picking me up. I'd a been out of luck in another five minutes.'

He replied, 'No problem.' He almost hadn't seen me. He asked if I lived in Virginia?

I told him, 'Yes sir. I teach school down there.'

He told me it was a tough job, and he didn't know if he would have the patience to do it.

I told him sometimes it was difficult. That there's a high burn-out rate among teachers. I told him I was actually up here helping a friend who is starting a new phase in his life, and then I asked him what brought him to upstate New York?"

The driver was pushing that Buick at around eighty miles an hour and he started telling me his story. It seems he'd gotten a call from an old girlfriend about three days before. She'd been in a wreck and was seriously injured. She was in the hospital and didn't have anyone else to call, so she'd called him. He had jumped in his car and come on up to New York as soon as he could.

I asked him how his girlfriend was and he said she would be okay even though she had a lot of rehab to do. He said she was one tough cookie. Now, the Buick was flying and that driver, he was expertly handling it through the light traffic.

I told him I was sure she was grateful he was able to come see her. He told me he almost didn't get a chance to see her.

I asked him what he meant as one set of headlights after another disappeared behind us.

Well, he told me the first night he got up here he was locked up. I was amazed that he would be telling me that, but it was going to be a long trip so I sat back to enjoy the story.

'Yep', he said. 'As you might be suspecting by now, I've got a heavy foot. I got a ticket for speeding and when the cop asked for my license, I couldn't find it. In my haste to get out of Atlanta and get up here as soon as I could, I left my billfold at home; my money, my I.D., my credit cards-all of it. I had maybe forty bucks cash in my pocket. That was all I brought up here with me.'

'So they locked you up?' I asked.

He said, 'That's right. They threw me in the drunk tank and wouldn't let me make a phone call until the next morning. They had no right in denying me my phone call to an attorney. Even the night court judge would not permit me to use the phone until the next morning. I was steaming, but there wasn't a thing I could do.'

Not only that, but they had confiscated the few possessions he'd had in his pockets, his cigarettes, and his money. And, his car was impounded. I told him I thought things like that only happened in the Deep South.

He replied, 'Evidently not.' He said he thought the cops were just doing their job, but that the night court judge had gone out of his way to make it tough on him. He told me the guys in the tank had treated him a lot better than the judge had. They gave him cigarettes and in general, kind of looked after him. But that judge, he just wouldn't listen. He told him all he needed was one call to his attorney in Atlanta and his identity would be cleared up and bail money would be wired immediately. But no, no, the judge wasn't in the mood to be treating him fairly which he said the twelve or fifteen guys in the drunk tank said was that judge's typical modus operandi. Said he had a reputation for being arrogant and mean.

Anyway the driver chuckled and continued, said he'd settled the score the next morning after they finally gave him his phone call. I guess he'd had a very influential attorney down in Atlanta. That lawyer was able to get the question of his identity cleared up and he had wired the money for his bail. He also got his car released. The driver had instructed him to also wire him enough cash to go the bail for those fifteen jail birds he'd spent the night with. The total bill was over thirty-five thousand dollars. I think some of those guys must have been in there for something a little more serious than drunk and disorderly. Anyway, he said it was worth it to see the look on the jailer's face when he peeled off them greenbacks and said he was paying bail for all fifteen of them. At first they said he couldn't do that. But his attorney must have anticipated as much and in a few minutes, that jail received a call from the New York State Attorney General in Albany. All his drunk-tank buddies were set free, and he said the jail house cops were more agitated than a bunch of caged up monkeys watching the third re-run of Planet of the Apes."

* * *

Toby set the novel aside and watched the threesome he'd noticed earlier. Now the black lady was showing the young couple snapshots from her billfold. "This is Reggie. He was a boxer. He went pro and won seven fights. Den' he got religion. Now he ah' family man and preachin' the Good

Book. And this is my baby, Rosie. She ain't got the religion like Reggie, but she's a good girl. God knows she a hard worker! She do most anything to make a dollah'." On and on she went; through all six of her children and then she came to a picture of her deceased husband. "Marvin was a fine man. Oh! He loved his children so very much. I sho' didn't think I'd make it when he passed on." The couple smiled at her, and the girl reached across and touched the black lady on the shoulder. Toby rested his head back and closed his eyes. He was wondering if and how a story about a hitchhiker and a trucker would connect with him. He realized that the truck driver thing was sort of an affirmation of his going to Memphis, but that was about all he could figure out at the moment. He picked the novel up and continued reading:

* * *

I told him I thought that was a great thing to do and that I thought those fellows he had bailed out wouldn't soon forget. He had slowed the Buick down for a speed zone in a town we were passing through, but when I looked at the speedometer, he was still ten miles per hour over the limit. I sat back and asked him if he had done anything like that before? He told me that he had actually done something crazier a few years ago. He said once again his attorney really earned his fee. He said he had a good friend who had made a few mistakes. As a result his friend ended up in a federal lock-up in West Tennessee. He said he was able to get in on a visitor pass about a year later and spent a half hour with him. The friend told him he was hanging tough, but although things were bad, he was coping. The friend told him that of all the things he missed, believe it or not, the thing he missed the most was chocolate candy. The friend had tried every way he could think of to get some chocolate candy smuggled in but nothing seemed to work. He told him he was going to die if he could not score some chocolate. The driver said he thought about it and then told his friend that he might have a plan. He asked him when was he allowed outside in the recreation yard.

The driver told me that he was a licensed pilot and kept a Lear Jet fueled and flight-ready, twenty-four seven. A month later he loaded it up with two hundred fifty cases of Snickers, Three Musketeers, and Hershey's Milk Chocolates. He said the load was around two thousand pounds. He had a helper on the flight open up the boxes. When he got over the prison recreation yard the helper pushed them all out the open cargo hatch. The driver laughed and said his prison friend later told him that the candy bars were so thick on the ground the men couldn't take a step without squashing a half dozen candy bars. He said every inmate in that recreation yard had stuffed the candy away and the guards actually encouraged them to do it. It was the only way they could get the mess cleaned up. He repeated that his attorney earned his fee on that little caper as he was not aware that there was a U. S. Navy air base at Millington Tennessee. He said he certainly was not aware of the fact that as he approached the penitentiary his altitude and bearing triggered two F-14 Phantoms to be scrambled to escort him out of the area. They actually had orders to intercept him before he flew over the prison, but they were late getting there. After he dropped his load of chocolate they came along side of him and ordered him to follow them back to Millington. I guess he had no idea that simply flying over a federal prison and dropping a little candy would have gotten him in so much trouble. He told me it took his attorney six months to restore his pilots license and get his jet out of the impound.

I had asked him what kind of work he did. I was intrigued with this modern day Robin Hood. He told me he was a trouble shooter for one of the large casinos in Las Vegas.

Since I didn't know what that meant, I asked.

He told me that when they get a player on a hot streak that seems to have a system that they can't figure out, they would give him a call. Now they wouldn't call if someone had just a few lucky plays. But if they had a pro that had really got it going; somebody that could break their bank, that's when they would call him in. That's why he kept the Lear Jet ready to go. When they call him, they expected him to be out there within three hours. In two or three hours they could lose a lot of money. He told me that they pay him well so it was worth the inconvenience when his services were requested.

I felt real awkward, but I was longing to ask him how much he was paid. I guess he'd had the question before because he seemed to anticipate it and told me that they pay guys like him usually around twenty thousand an hour. He said he was on the clock the second he walked through the door until the job was done. He said that there were only two or three guys who commanded that kind of pay and confided that the other two were only asked to work if for some reason he couldn't be there himself.

I asked him what he did when he got there, and he told me that he would sit in at the table and get a feel for what type of con the player is running. The player might be solo, or he could be part of a team. He said there could be lots of things that could be going on. A lot of troubleshooters can spot a good con going down. His specialty though was sitting in on a player who has a mathematical system working which is seemingly undefeatable. He said there are only a couple of people who have success at stopping a player like that.

I asked him what his secret was, and he said it wasn't a secret. The thing he had going was a talent for remembering numbers or sequences of numbers.

I asked him if he meant that because he could remember numbers he was able to figure out a mathematical gambling system. He told me there was a little more to it than that, but, yes, that was most of it. When he said he could remember numbers, he meant he could remember all numbers. He could retrieve every number he'd ever seen in his life. He could remember his grandmother's street number forty years ago or the lock combination on his eighth grade junior high school locker. He remembered a pretty girl in math class when he was seven. He would glance over her shoulder to see the long division problems she was working on, and he could still tell you every number on that page. In short, he had a photographic memory for numbers. He'd always had it.

There it was. I knew there was something special about that guy. I told him that I guessed they had run a zillion tests on him to figure out how he had received the gift. He told me that the skill wasn't necessarily a gift, that sometimes it was a curse. He said he had not been tested but was convinced that his parents giving him cards when he was a baby in the crib was the cause. The earliest thing he remembered in life was the numbers on those cards. Ever since then, there had not been one number or sequence of numbers that he couldn't retrieve.

I was amazed and impressed. I could see why he would be good in a gambling environment. And then I asked him, if, when he wasn't doing his thing on the clock for the casino operators in Vegas, did he play cards for recreation? He told me he'd been known to play a little poker now and then. I bet that he had played with some of the really high rollers. He allowed as he had."

* * *

Toby again laid the paperback down and stretched his body as best he could. He looked out the windows and watched the southland of America pass by. How many slaves had worked these fields a hundred and fifty years ago? He wondered how many of their great-great grandchildren now held bachelor, masters, and doctorate degrees? What was it about America that could see this change occur? Toby wasn't sure exactly what it was, but he loved it. He knew that! He loved seeing oppressed people finally standing strong. He loved whatever it was that helps them do it. He knew that in a lot of places around the world it would never happen. But here in America it has happened. No, he thought, the U.S.A. isn't perfect. There are still a lot of problems; still a lot of injustices; still plenty of racial hatred; still corruption; and plenty of moral backsliding. Despite all of these persistent problems, America was a place that the hope for justice, the hope for a better way of life remained strong.

Toby knew as long as Americans were willing to sacrifice and to fight that America would continue to be the bastion for human hope. In Toby's mind, that was exactly the current problem. He was afraid that too many Americans were no longer willing to sacrifice and fight. America's soft underbelly was being more and more exposed. The events of 9-11 were inevitable, and in Toby's mind they were only the first step towards more damaging attacks sure to be launched by the Muslim extremist. He felt that Al-Qaeda and others were totally cognizant of the fact that most Americans were more concerned about their stock portfolios and their bowling scores than they were about a radical Muslim element perhaps two million strong that openly threatened to totally reduce America to ashes.

Toby agreed with those who felt that America had never been more polarized than it was now. Americans were split perfectly down the middle on a whole list of issues that were well known and openly debated before 9-11. On one side were the anti-war, pro abortion, pro gay, anti school prayer, anti ten commandments, environmental doomsayers. On the other side were the pro military, pro life, pro family, pro God, pro free market economy with limited government and low taxes crowd. Toby was rightfully concerned that this polarization would, now, after 9-11, only increase to a dangerous level; a level that would threaten institutional break down. His fears were not his alone. Many across the country on both sides of the ever increasing chasm had the same fears. He gazed out the window. America. What does it really mean? Who are her children? What is her destiny? Has 'In God We Trust' been reduced to a feeble cliché? Or, are there folks left who will sacrifice and fight? The Greyhound Bus rolled down the road, over rivers, through small towns, by schools, churches, cemeteries, and railroad tracks. He knew there were stretches of land where he was now traveling that would absolutely soothe a weary man's soul. There were places just a few miles from this highway that would bathe a worried man in the beauty and fragrance of its spring. There were places that would allow him to rest and cool in a clear stream in the summer or encourage him to walk among the color of the autumn forest on a brisk and windy afternoon. There were places that would be a cocoon for him and his woman, where they could be naked and unashamed on the floor in front of their woodstove in winter. Toby loved this land. He loved America.

The black lady two rows in front of him was sleeping peacefully, her head slumped to her left shoulder. The young white couple was also sleeping and holding hands. Toby opened the paperback again.

* * *

"The miles whizzed by. I expected to see blue police lights at any moment. This guy really had a thing for speed. But other than speed, he was a good driver. We crossed over into Virginia from Maryland and stopped for gas. While we were waiting he popped open his trunk and showed me a lot of confiscated items the casinos had taken from cheating gamblers. There were all kinds of loaded dice, card markers, tiny ear-phones for a two man con, infra-red lenses, even drugs and chemicals a cheater would try to slip into other players' drinks.

We were approaching my home town off I-81 in Virginia and I told him that I sure appreciated the ride. I told him it was an experience I wouldn't soon forget. I was thinking that I couldn't wait to get home and tell my wife about him. As thanks for the ride, I asked him if he would join me for a pizza or something.

I was surprised when he said, 'Sure. I'm getting hungry. I'd be happy to accept.'

We went in a pizza restaurant just off I-81. I phoned my wife to come pick me up. While we waited and ate, I had an impulse I just could not make go away. I told him that everything he'd told me had impressed me tremendously. It wasn't everyday I meet somebody like him. The stories he told, everything. There was one idea that was floating around in my head. I asked him if he would play a game of liar's poker with me. I was thinking how I'd love to tell the teachers at school that I played a real high roller. He agreed, for a dollar. We both laughed. Then we each produced a dollar bill and exchanged them for two 'clean' ones from the waitress. I shuffled them and offered them face down towards the Las Vegas casino troubleshooter, who was probably the best gambler in the world. He drew one and made two folds in the bill and brought it up towards his eyes. I did the same with my bill. I asked him if he wanted to open, or if he wanted me to go first. He said he was cool either way.

'All rightee. Let me see, I'll go with a pair of three's.'

The troubleshooter said, 'pair of sixes.'

I said, 'pair of eights.'

He came back with, 'pair of nines.'

I was trying to get the feel again. It had been ten years since I'd last played liars poker. I decided to bluff my two treys to three, hoping he would have one. 'Three treys,' I said.

The troubleshooter, not so quickly, came back with, 'Three nines.'

My instincts were to call the three nines. I didn't have any to support the likely bluff. But instead I went with my hidden deuces. 'Four deuces.'

He called. I smiled and opened the bill. I had three deuces and with the deuce from his bill, I won, and collected his dollar bill. I felt great. I had just beaten a casino bigwig. Then I heard six words that would be etched in my memory for a long time; words I have repeated a thousand times whenever I tell this story.

The troubleshooter with a voice as smooth as silk and possessing the spirit of a leopard pouncing a doomed antelope asked me, 'Do you want to play again?' "

* * *

The Greyhound would be approaching the Memphis area in another hour. Toby's thoughts drifted from the paperback novel to the two week crash course in truck driving that would start tomorrow. What kind of challenges awaited him? Before he could think of any, a silent alarm went off in his head and the *big question* returned – the question most folks find themselves asking sooner or later. *Who am I?* The question had haunted Toby all his life. As a young boy he remembered playing war games; the Japs against the G.I.'s; cowboys and Indians; anything to get into the woods or cornfields and do battle. Elaborate forts and hideouts would be built and defending them from rock and BB-gun attacks was life itself. Back then it was a natural thing to do. Politically correct posturing hadn't been created yet. All the children's fathers had fought in WW II or Korea. Kids nowadays don't play those games, Toby thought, at least not with the intensity and pure black and white moral affirmation shown by the kids in the fifties.

Back then, his aunts and both grandmothers would often lay the syrupy, soft, southern, feminine affection on him. He had one aunt so confectionary that she could make a boy throw-up. She would pull him to her and overwhelm him with the gooiest stream of platitudinous praise and flatteries. "Toby you are just the sweetest child. Come here honey, Aunt Effie is going to love you, and love you; you sweet darling child." Aunt Effie meant well but only had one method of conveying love and affection which was to his young mind, suffocation. Toby had asked himself, *Who am I? A soldier or a little girly-boy?*

He remembered one day at the very young age of four, he was playing with neighbor children. Their father was opening up the crawl space under his house and was preparing to drag some tools under the house with him to repair some plumbing. Toby and the man's children wanted to help. The man said, "You can pass these tools on to me." They did so. When the man couldn't budge a rusty joint with his wrenches, he let out a viscous stream of profanities. Toby, thinking he was now the man's confidant, after all the help he'd been providing, tried his meager four year-old best to duplicate the profanities. The man screamed at him instantly with, "Little boy, don't you *ever* let me hear you say those words again." Toby was, of course, thoroughly deflated, but more than that, he was confused. *Who am I?* An adult's friend and ally, or an insect to be squashed? That *big question* reoccurred frequently from elementary school and on into the tenth grade.

Then something happened one night that eliminated many

possibilities about who Toby might be. In a corn field scuffle with a rival gang of teen age red necks, Toby and his best friend tackled a boy a year younger than they were. Toby's best friend held the younger boy down and Toby grabbed the hair of the boy's head and pulled the head back, stretching the neck to the max. Toby laid the blade of an eighteen inch long Bowie knife across the boys neck and said, "If you move an inch, I'll cut your throat." He really would not have done it, but the boy didn't know that. The boy cried, and it really was a bad scene. From then on Toby knew for sure he wasn't a Momma's boy.

Now, as the Greyhound approached Memphis, another question invaded the clutter of his consciousness. *What am I doing?* From the night of the three shooting stars, two things had been clear. He was a soldier. And he was preparing for a battle of some kind. He would take his training and await his orders. Toby didn't possess the character trait of second guessing the important decisions he had made throughout his life. He wasn't second guessing this one either. He believed God was in control and felt He was directing him towards the action that had crossed his mind that night in September.

No, he wasn't second guessing, but he sure was thinking about how it would all play out.

Chapter Five

The Greyhound was nearing Memphis, and Toby didn't know when he would get another chance to read. He picked up where he'd left off earlier.

* * *

The truck driver had just come to the end of his story when the CB cut in with..."Don't you forget that! That's right truck driver. I was there. I was there when Jesus was in the manger. I was one of the three who had traveled a great distance on the camels. And yes, we praised the Holy Child. Yes again! I was there when John the Baptist baptized Jesus."

The hitchhiker snickered and glanced over at the truck driver. They were still in the wide open spaces of West Texas and had somehow come across this strange voice on the CB radio.

"He sure *sounds* like he knows what he's talking about," the truck driver said to the hitchhiker.

"His voice does have a quality, a certain ring to it. I will grant him that much," the hitchhiker said.

The CB voice they were hearing was a solitary voice. The other drivers he was in conversation with, *If there were other drivers*, thought the hitchhiker, must have been out of range. All he and the truck driver heard was a one sided conversation. It was almost like hearing someone talking to themselves. There was a pause of ten or twenty seconds of air wave static between the things he said.

The truck driver looked at the hitchhiker, winked and keyed his CB microphone. He said, "Break one-nine. Where's the driver that was with Baby Jesus at the manger? Give me a come-back."

Nothing. The strange CB voice was quoting various biblical scripture presumably to other unheard drivers. The truck driver continued trying to get a come-back, and finally, "Yes, I copy you, friend. What can I do for you?"

"I heard you say you were there when the Baby Jesus was in the manger."

"That's right. That's exactly what I said."

"Hmmmm. That would be just about two thousand years ago. How is that possible?" The truck driver knew perfectly well how it was possible but led the other CB voice along for a specific purpose.

The strange CB voice took on a tone of total confidence and authority; the kind of tone and feeling that made you want to believe what he said. "Driver, let me assure you, all things on this Earth are in control of The Heavenly Father. He sends his angels to protect and watch over humans, and sometimes to intervene in awesome ways. Then again, sometimes in seemingly insignificant ways. But do not forget this! With God all things are possible."

The hitchhiker was clearly agitated and nearly jerked the CB mike out of the truck driver's hand. He caught himself and settled back but gestured for the mike. The truck driver handed it over to him. He had a lot more questions he wanted to lead the strange CB voice with, but also figured it would be wise to give the hitchhiker a shot at the voice.

The hitchhiker keyed the mike and asked the question, "Are you saying that you are an angel?"

"We are all angels. Read your bible. We are all the one third of the heavenly angels kicked out by God-Almighty. It's our punishment to be here on Earth. It's all in The Word. God spelled it out. Those who are so clouded by the flesh that they won't study The Word are in peril. It's all in The Book. Read Revelation. What a magnificent way for The Father to show us what will surely take place for us all."

The hitchhiker wasn't snickering now. It wasn't because the strange CB voice had awakened any slumbering Christian faith. No, it was because the voice captivated him. He simply was mesmerized by the power of the voice. And so it was for the truck driver as well. Even though the truck driver had had many conversations over the years with those that were like him.

The truck driver took the mike back, "Mister, I'm just a plain ol' truck driver. I work hard. I try to respect people. I don't get foul mouthed or ornery on the CB. I wish I could -he was going to say believe you, because he was still attempting to lead the strange CB voice, but he was cut off.

"Driver your companion has a good heart. He may or may not want to be Godly. Wanting to and doing it aren't the same. Only The Lamb will know if his name will be in the Book of Life. I have been on Earth since 1507. I have had twenty-one lives. All of these years men have tried to prove me crazy. I've been diagnosed delusional, paranoid, bi-polar, schizophrenic, you name it. What ever new slick mental disease comes along will be used to label me. Of course it's just their effort to deny the truth, and to delay God's final judgment."

The hitchhiker asked, incredulously, "Did you say 1507? You've been here since 1507? I thought you said you were here when Jesus was born. Twenty-one lives. Let's see now... You were with Jesus. That would be one life. You are now a truck driver. That would be two lives. What do you remember about the other nineteen lives?"

The hitchhiker never got an answer from the strange, captivating voice claiming to be a fallen angel. Instead he turned the conversation back at the truck driver and the hitchhiker. "It's not about me. Don't delude yourself. Every man will have to answer to the judgment. I could tell you things you would probably never believe. Jesus told us that 'The Son of Man will send out His angels, and they will gather out of His kingdom all things that offend, and those who practice lawlessness, and will cast them into the furnace of fire. There will be wailing and gnashing of teeth. Then the righteous will shine forth as the sun in the kingdom of their Father. He who has ears to hear, let him hear!'"

The strange CB voice paused, then came back, "There is no need for me to explain my mission, my steadfast loyalty to The Lamb. I just told you what must be done. If you have ears, Jesus said, 'Let him hear.' He also tells us there will be those that do not hear." The last few words faded. And at the end they heard only the cacophony of CB skip.

The driver tried to reach the speaker again, but there was no come-back. "I guess we lost him." A comfortable silence ensued. It seemed each man had some thinking to do.

The hitchhiker sat back, folded his arms and pretended to sleep. His eyes were closed but his mind spun as he thought about some of the strange things the CB voice had said. Other than the fallen angel thing and the Jesus stuff, it wasn't all that different from some things he himself had thought about and been involved with years ago: spirits, time travel, etc. No, he certainly couldn't sit there and condemn the strange CB voice for possibly being a crackpot. *How long had it been since he'd pondered on these things? Twenty-five years?*

He remembered the night Maggie first turned him on to dope – Sweet Mary Jane. He had resisted Maggie's efforts for a couple of months, but then that one night he had smoked that joint with her and everything changed. A young ex Marine living in Hawaii he had somehow managed to escape all the other invitations to step over the threshold from the straight world into the psychedelic world. Most of his friends and co-workers were into it. They had many times invited him to smoke dope with them. He had always been able to rely on his conviction that the saying was true, "Just a one time experiment with drugs could be enough to get you hooked." That statement he had always respected.

Sure, he, like everyone else saw the footage of the Hippies, Haight Ashbury, and Woodstock. What was the harm everyone said? If smoking a little grass helped young people relieve some stress. If it helped just a little to briefly escape from the gone mad world of Viet Nam, nuclear holocaust, the military industrial complex – what's the harm?

Back in those days his nickname had been Windjammer. So long ago. He couldn't remember the last time he'd had anyone call him Windjammer. Then he had watched society make all those justifications for the innocent use of a little herb. But he never bought it. He never succumbed to the temptation and pressure to get tuned in and turned on. Not until the night Maggie had finally got to him.

She was twenty-eight, a pure hot-blooded vixen if ever there was one. Five years Windjammer's senior in chronology, but ages his senior in worldly ways, especially sex. She controlled him thoroughly. He was undoubtedly an eager student, and he thought he'd learned about all there was to know. That night she lit the incense, the candles, showed him how to inhale the sweet weed, and cooked him a fabulous meal. After his first toke he thought *'this stuff taste like a bad cigarette. What's the big deal?'* After his second toke he sensed a slight tingling in his extremities, not much more. After his third toke a pleasant light headed feeling began to break down all the taboos he'd used to stay away from the dangerous weed.

Maggie was pleased. Now she really had him. They were in the kitchen and laughing hugely, Windjammer thought, at the strangest things. Maggie helped him see things he'd never seen before. An ordinary skillet with its varying shades of grays and blacks became the unmistakable face of Black Beard the pirate. The yellow wall took on the appearance of a golden sunset on the beach. Windjammer was amazed at all the little things in an ordinary room he had been missing until this night. They laughed and laughed, and when finally the sex began, Windjammer knew he had *not* learned all Maggie had to teach him.

A bump in the road interrupted his reflection. He sat up and stretched. He looked toward the driver, but he seemed either lost in thought or mesmerized by the green light from the dash. Windjammer returned both to his position and his thoughts. *This CB guy says he is an angel and is here to warn us about the judgment. Who knows? Twenty-five years ago, the night Maggie turned me on the first time, the door was opened to my own spirituality.* Windjammer thought his experiences and those of strange CB voice were spiritually very similar. He could not have been further from the truth.

* * *

The Greyhound pulled into the terminal in Memphis. Toby watched the young white couple and the black lady say their good byes, and then they melted into the disheveled throngs of travelers and every stripe of misplaced poor. There was an hour before the Mountaintop Transport van would pick him up, so he set out to walk and get a little exercise.

He walked through a very nice city park. Fall color was ablaze in the oaks. The flower gardens and shrubs were not, as yet, harmed by any early frost. There was a huge statue of General Nathan Bedford Forrest, one of the Confederates most daring and dashing leaders. His cavalry raids on Union troops were legendary. A Tennessee native, Forrest seemingly toyed with much larger union forces and to this day is viewed by some as the "should have been" commander of all Confederate forces. Today he sat atop a splendid war horse, reins in hand gazing towards the Mississippi River looking as if he were ready to come to life again and lead the South to glory. Toby felt a twinge of southern pride run through him. He thought, *there's the kind of man we need today – an invincible leader, unafraid, ready at a moments notice to strike the enemy.* He hoped he would be able to gather what was needed to become a soldier such as Nathan Bedford Forrest had been a hundred and thirty-seven years ago. He walked on towards the river, veered south a couple of blocks and found himself on Beale Street. He wasn't in the mood for the Mardi Gras-like street scene that was carefully tweaked and managed by the City of Memphis. He turned and headed back toward the Greyhound station. The company van would be there in twenty minutes. Tomorrow at seven a.m. he would be the oldest rookie wannabe truck driver in the class of fifty other wannabe truck drivers. He would also be the most dedicated and the most dangerous.

Chapter Six

Toby worked hard the next two weeks to learn all he could. Most of the time was allotted to the driving range on the Mountaintop Transport training facility. After breakfast the trainees would be on the range behind the wheel with a trainer either in the cab with them or outside watching closely. Towards the end of the two week period they would venture outside the gates onto the Memphis city streets. Days with horrible weather were usually set aside for indoor book training – weight and load distribution, map reading, trip planning, and the filling out of logs and forms.

The paper back novel had caught Toby's attention. Every night, when the others went out for beer, Toby followed Windjammer, the hitchhiker, and the truck driver all through West Texas and into New Mexico. He still hadn't discovered a message for himself, if there was one to be found, but the story was interesting. Whatever spare moments he could get, he read.

* * *

The moon was nearly full. The truck driver had pulled the rig off the highway into a broad turn-out where two other eighteen wheelers had decided to call it a night. It was after eleven p.m. They had stopped at a diner earlier. The truck driver had insisted that he would treat them both to a good meal. Windjammer had made no protest. It was shortly before they had stopped to eat that the signal on the CB from the fallen angel had faded away. Neither one of them had said much about it. The truck driver only suggested that it was just one more nutcase he could add to the many he had heard over the years. Inwardly he was thanking the Heavenly Father for sending the strange CB voice. It would hopefully help open the door to Windjammer's heart. He wasn't exactly sure at this stage as to how he himself would proceed on that task. Surely he would proceed, but on this particular mission he thought it best to go slowly. Hopefully Windjammer would open up on his own. Windjammer had nothing outwardly to say, but on the inside he was thinking about the strange CB. voice and the memories of twenty-five years ago that voice had triggered.

The truck driver had slipped into the lower bunk in the sleeper berth and had offered Windjammer the upper bunk. Tomorrow they would easily make Flagstaff before the sun set and Windjammer would be back on the highway hitching his way on to California. Before trying to slip off to sleep, Windjammer did what he did every night. He silently recited his 'code of the road.'

Wind spirit blow through me again

May I be like disappearing vapor

No pain, no ties, no memories

Only tomorrow.

*Laughter, the road, and anticipation will
be my companions*

No pain, no ties, no memories

Only tomorrow

Sleep would eventually come for Windjammer tonight, but contrary to the dictates of his road code, he did have memories; memories twenty-five years old. His memories of that time in his life could be catalogued under five major headings: traveling with good looking women, traveling alone, drinking and drugging with good looking women, drinking and drugging alone, and surfing. Another three sub headings would include delving into Eastern religion and philosophy, the occult, and war memories from Viet Nam. When his memory bank exploded into action, all eight of these categories would be reviewed, but in no particular order; and sometimes, simultaneously.

Tonight's voyage through the confusing waters of time-gone-by started with the voluptuous and treacherous Maggie. Poor Maggie. He had come to think of her more as a victim of the flawed relationship than he had been. As she drew him deeper into her web of lust and deceit he gradually but with no uncertainty lost most of his small town innocence, and a good part of his soul. The weeks went on. They smoked more grass together and got into a heavy sexual routine flavored by Maggie's compulsion to lean towards the kinky.

Three months later she dumped Windjammer for his boss. A couple of years later Maggie's fast life style caught up with her. She was a basket case alcoholic and heavy into drugs. She was lucky that several Nuns had picked her up and were trying to sober her up. By this time Windjammer's graduation from the basic sex and drug education she had given him had developed into his own graduate level thesis on the subjects. He sought her out one night and was shocked by her condition. That didn't deter him from making a pass that she wanted no part of. It was really very sad for both of them. Maggie was in no condition to do anything, and Windjammer's judgment, wisdom, and morals had been so reduced he couldn't see it.

More women came in and out of his life. His love for surfing grew. He experimented with transcendental meditation, Zen, and Hawaiian spiritualism. He had built up an extensive list of drugs he played with after his introduction to marijuana: cocaine, acid, opium, elephant tranquilizer, peyote, and mescaline. The crowd he ran in was a very fast crowd. Many were Hollywood rejects or has-beens. They frequently came to Hawaii hoping to hit it off with another phony who actually had some real money. Others were ex military, like himself, drawn to Oahu's beaches for the surfing, the free and easy life style, and preying on the summertime co-ed traffic.

There was one ex military type that wanted Windjammer to go into business with him. The night the man introduced himself, Windjammer was tending bar at The Ramparts. "What's your pleasure?" Windjammer asked the man who had taken the last barstool down at the end. Windjammer hated that. He always liked to keep that bar stool open for the date he many times would score near the end of his eight hour shift. Down there, twenty feet away from the pouring station, he could talk to girls more or less in private.

"Bourbon rocks, splash of soda."

"Got it," Windjammer deftly slid a cocktail napkin in front of the man and walked back to pour the drink.

Teresa, a strikingly beautiful Malaysian, Norwegian, French, mix of a woman waited for him on her side of the bar at the cocktail waitress station.

"Order," she said.

"Just a second, sweetheart." Windjammer poured the man's drink, returned to the end of the bar, placed it on the cocktail napkin in front of the man. He got back to Teresa. She was one of the few women that worked in or hung around the Ramparts that he couldn't get to. "Whatcha' got?"

"Jack water, Cutty soda, Vodka Collins, two salty dogs, one mai tai, and two drafts," she said quickly and ignored the glassy eyed stares of two submarine sailors sitting at the bar next to the cocktail waitress station.

"Got it," Windjammer said and had the order on her tray in less than forty-five seconds.

Bimbette and Bambi were the next waitresses to place their orders. When they weren't cocktailing in Waikiki they roomed together in Manoa Valley near the University of Hawaii where they both had been studying on and off for three years. Bimbette was a pretty blond from Oregon, and Bambi was a gorgeous happa-haole (pidgin English for a mixed local and Caucasian). Only a week ago Windjammer and the two girls had crashed Bambi's Mustang on their way home from a bar hopping binge. Windjammer took full advantage of Bambi's condition that night and had slipped into bed with her for the first time.

After placing the girl's drinks on their trays, Windjammer stepped back towards the cash register on the back bar, lit a cigarette, inhaled deeply, and surveyed the scene this Thursday night at the popular Ramparts Bar in the heart of world famous Waikiki Beach. A slow crowd so far, he thought, but it will pick up when the two-man guitar act get it cranked up. The room was small. Fifty customers was a maximum crowd, and The Ramparts achieved those numbers most nights. Would tonight be any different? Probably not. The same crowd would show up. Tourists and locals as well would come in to relax, to try to get lucky, to fill the emptiness of their lives with alcohol. An hour from now the eight bar stools nearest the waitress station would be filled with the "regulars". Windjammer would make their drink when he saw them come in the door across the room, where the bouncer passed them through the line at the door. In the bar scene you couldn't get any higher form of respect than that. But it was slow now. Windjammer only had three customers sitting at the bar in front of him and that bourbon rocks splash soda guy down at the end. He glanced that way and saw the man's glass was empty. He walked down and said, "Ready for another?"

"Good idea," the man said. Then, "I saw you at Waiamea last week. That last wave you dropped in on. Wow!! I gotta' tell you. That was the wildest thing I have ever seen!"

All of his co-workers and the regulars knew about Windjammer's reputation as a big wave surfer on the North Shore, but rarely would an ordinary tourist recognize him. Maybe this guy was not an ordinary tourist. It caught Windjammer off guard, "Uh, yeah, well, yeah, that was an unusual ride. I wasn't sure I was going to make it happen."

"Oh you are just being modest. There aren't ten people on the planet that could have pulled that off. Let's face it, you're a guy that will take chances."

Windjammer talked with the man for a minute or two, then avoided any further conversation. He was glad to see him leave a half hour later.

The night wore on. The guitar guys had the crowd revved up with Sloop John B. Windjammer stepped outside for a ten minute break. A fellow bartender at the Ramparts on his night off stood in for him. Windjammer walked around the corner to Kalakaua Ave., then down a block and walked into another bar. He found the man he was looking for but first said to the bartender, "Hey Pete, what's up?"

"How's it 'Jammer?" and Pete went back to his conversation with someone else.

Windjammer sat down next to Bill Finch. "I heard you got into a big Blue Fin off Maile Point." Finch was a stocky sunburned Pennsylvania Dutch who operated a thirty foot charter fishing boat in his off duty time. On duty, he was a Lieutenant in the U. S. Navy working out of the Office of Naval Intelligence at Pearl Harbor.

"We were lucky. I had no idea that size fish was out there. My customer gave me a $500 tip."

"Billy, sometimes I think you are the luckiest squid in all of paradise, but listen, I've got a favor to ask."

"Shoot."

"A guy came in the Ramparts a little while ago. Something just didn't jive with his story. I want to ask you to check around a little and see if you can come up with anything."

Finch owed Windjammer a favor or two and said he'd do what he could. But he needed more to go on. "So what do you think his story might be?"

Windjammer lit a cigarette and said, "He'd been hanging around the North Shore the last month or so watching the action. Nothing unusual, but then he said he had a business proposition for me and I'd be able to make some big money." He waited for effect.

"Go on," Bill Finch said.

"There was something about him. I think he might be a spook."

Billy lifted his eyebrows a little, "A spook here in paradise? Can you imagine that," he said, sarcasm oozing.

"I know if anybody could get a fix on him, it'd be you. I gotta' get back. I hope you sneak up on another big Blue Fin. Oh yeah, he said his name was Richard Loeffler."

Windjammer got to his feet and turned to leave, but Finch latched on to his arm. "Did you say Richard Loeffler?"

"Yeah, that's what he said."

Finch lifted his eyebrows even higher this time. "I won't need to do any checking on this guy. You said he wants to make you a business deal?"

Windjammer nodded yes and was already reading the worry in Finch's face.

"Jammer, your Joe tourist, who just happens to be a big wave surf fan? He *is* a spook, or at least he used to be. You remember when Saigon fell and the choppers were evacuating people off the roof of the embassy?"

"Sure, it was all over TV."

"Right. Well, Richard Loeffler was the highest ranking CIA agent left in Saigon that last day. The scuttlebutt was that nobody got anywhere near the roof of that embassy unless they had gone through Loeffler. I've heard estimates that he pocketed a couple of million bucks. He has been popping up here in the islands on a regular basis for about a year and a half now. My guess would be that he's trying to recruit you to look after a pot growing operation he has tucked away in a valley over on the windward side."

"Why me?"

"Two reasons, I'd say. He probably thinks you've got the balls to do it. And secondly, his last manager up there was killed four days ago."

Jammer sat back down. "He had a guy working for him that got killed? What happened."

"My sources say the guy was ex marine, gone local, and gone mad on weed. He had a lot in common with you. Anyway some of the Mokes over there on the windward side went into the plantation one night to rip off as much weed as they could. Willis was the guy's name. He confronted them. He probably thought they would turn and back off, but one of the Mokes put a jungle spear right through his heart. His days of hemp security ended right there. Listen Jammer, if I were you, I'd stay as far away from Loeffler as I possibly could."

* * *

One evening about half way through the two week driver training course, Toby went across the street to a family diner. He had been reading while he slowly ate his meal, when he was interrupted. Two other trainees in his class came in and joined him at his booth. "Whatcha reading, Etheridge? You got a good skin book?"

"No, no it's not that." From what he'd seen so far, most of the trainees he'd been working with were very limited in any social graces. Obscenities, profanities and a crudeness that he could only remember from his old Navy days seemed to be the medium that some truckers and wannabe truckers conversed in. To be perfectly honest, he had to admit that it was easy for him to be led down that same treacherous path to the pit of filthy language they seemed to wallow in. He constantly had to guard against slipping into that ugly hole. He wasn't always successful, but this time he tactfully changed the direction of the conversation. "Hey, did I see you guys talking to that tanker driver across the road?"

"Sure was. He was telling us about an accident he eyeballed just about a week ago."

"What did he have to say?" Toby laid the book aside and waited for them to continue.

"Well, it was pretty hairy, I guess. I wouldn't want to go out like that. He told us he was coming down the hill, eastbound, where Highway 40 crosses the Tennessee river. He saw a big truck directly in front of him lose control and hit the outside wall."

The other trainee jumped in, as anxious as the first to retell the rest of the story. They were both glowing. After all, an experienced driver with over twenty years on the road, had just shared a real life truck story with them. In a way they were already part of that boundless reservoir of trucking mythology because an old hand shared his story with them. And it was true. Truckers didn't talk about these things to just anybody – only those in the brotherhood or in the case of these guys, those about to join the brotherhood. "That's right! He told us the truck hit the wall and the right side fuel tank blew up on impact. It was still dragging along the wall and fire was all over the place. The driver of the other truck just couldn't pull it back to the middle. He said it must have gone two hundred and fifty feet on that wall 'til finally the tractor, trailer, the whole damn thing just went all the way over."

The trainee paused for emphasis which was a mistake. The first trainee jumped back in as narrator. "The tanker driver said an article in the paper came out yesterday about that truck jumping the rail and falling in the river. The tractor was found three days later two miles downstream, but the trailer was right there under the bridge. Now, how do you think that could have happened?"

Now the time was ripe for all kinds of unnecessary and useless speculation. The second trainee pounced on the opening left for him. "That must be one hell of a current. Two miles downstream!"

The first trainee didn't give him the opportunity to elaborate. "I think I know what happened. I'm pretty sure there were two big ol' channel cats down there just swimming around. You know, the two hundred pounders. When they seen that dead driver in that cab come drifting down to the bottom, they chained up to the tractor and pulled it downstream. Why, hells bells! They were presented with a golden opportunity to bring a good meal to all them little baby catfish they had waitin' on them."

Toby couldn't resist getting his two cents worth in. "No, I don't think that's what happened. I think that driver had his foot jammed down on the throttle. When the tractor separated from the trailer and made it to the bottom, well, he just kept at it. That old tractor must have kept churning up the muddy bottom of that river for another two miles." While Toby did avoid the profanity and obscene language trap, he later realized that he had fallen into the trap of disrespecting the dead driver. He knew, however, that light hearted joking and laughing about the violent and untimely death of other truck drivers was actually a psychological release valve. It was one way to deal with the considerable pressure all truck drivers deal with, the contemplation of their own deaths. They laughed at it. It was the same release valve many combat veterans used.

A little later the two trainees headed out the door of the restaurant. They were loud, obnoxious and did their best to let everyone in the place know they were about to become over-the-road big rig drivers. They were young and green. Toby knew he was green too, but time had seasoned him enough to listen more and speak less. Although he didn't show it, inwardly, Toby was a little disappointed with the quality of men who were in his training class. Perhaps the difference was that the others were looking for something to do, while he was using this training to help him do something. Toby's trucking future was tied to a mission he felt God had directed him to execute. This was a mission which, he hoped, would protect America from more attacks or possibly exact retribution on the forces responsible for 9–11.

Toby looked down at the ragged paperback. He felt that it contained something that would help him with his fourth decision. What it might be, he didn't know. He only knew that he was inexorably drawn to it. He continued reading.

Chapter Seven

Windjammer lay there in the top bunk somewhere in New Mexico, thinking about Maggie, Bimbette, Bambi, The Ramparts, Finch, Loeffler, and Willis. Ron Willis was the kid whose sneakers were always untied, and his worn out shirts were hand me downs from three brothers above him. His mother was half Cherokee and his father was a motorcycle gangster before the Hells Angels were ever dreamed of.

Windjammer had seen Ron Willis in knife fights by the time the boy was fifteen.

By the time he was seventeen he toted a .38 snub nose for protection from the patrons of the rough bars he played in around St. Louis. Willis was the drummer. Windjammer knew most of the others in the band, 'The Shadows', but he didn't hang with them. He was way too busy playing football, basketball, baseball, and being the leading man in the school plays.

Windjammer was better friends with Ron Willis's brother Randolf, known in their inner circle as Froggy, than he was with Ron. The working class neighborhood they all grew up in was on the outskirts of St. Louis. Tough red necks were in their backyards and tough

Irish Catholics in the front yard. Gang mentality wasn't what it would soon become, but it was real enough to Jammer and the four Willis brothers. Many were the fights they found themselves in, and many times they found themselves protecting each other and looking out for each other.

Ron Willis was a boy you learned to expect to be involved in violence. Jammer remembered the day the two of them played stick hockey with an old rusty beer can on a frozen pond. No skates, just shoes, cold fingers, snot dripping, and playing one on one hockey. When Jammer declared himself the winner, Ron picked up his BB gun and put two stinging BB's in Jammer's thighs. Ron said, "If you don't want two more in your eyes, you'll get down on the ground like the dog you are." Jammer was down quick. Ron made him crawl all the way home on all fours keeping the BB gun aimed at his rear end.

There were good times too. Lot's of them. But, Ron did not graduate high school. Instead he joined the Marines two months before he turned eighteen. Windjammer had played one year of college football, then he enlisted after he'd seen Ron come home on leave, sparkling and shining in his starched, razor creased dress blues. From then on it seemed like Windjammer was always six months behind Ron Willis. Six months after Ron's infantry unit went to Viet Nam, Windjammer's infantry unit did the same. They never crossed paths in Viet Nam but on two occasions

Windjammer heard Marines from other units in the E. M. club tell stories about a Lance Corporal named Ron Willis. According to them Willis was the reason many of them were still alive. Story after story supported his reputation as a relentless, brutal killer of V.C. and N.V.A. After awhile the American commanders were all clamoring to pull him out of his unit and assign him to some special mission they were planning. After Lance Corporal Willis had completed his tour he was assigned security duty at the Kaneohe Marine Corps Air Station on Oahu.

Six months later Windjammer followed him to Oahu but was assigned to security duty at Pearl Harbor.

When Willis was discharged from the marines he went home to St. Louis only to realize he would never fit in that environment again. He went back to Oahu and picked up on his drums where he had left off — cheap jobs in dingy bar rooms. The only thing added to the mix this time were drugs by the bucket-full and the exotic women of Polynesia.

Windjammer's return to St. Louis as a civilian after the marines was equally as disappointing. Everything seemed so small - the houses, the neighborhood, the opportunities, the people. Yes, the people were small. They were seemingly content to work factory jobs, drive beer trucks, raise three kids, pay the mortgage, and all the rest. Windjammer's return to Oahu was, for him, a joyous reunion with the ocean. He missed it terribly in the four months he stayed in St. Louis. But now he was back and nothing, not even drugs or women, kept him out of the ocean. In his first months back he and Ron Willis got together on a regular basis. Some time later, after Windjammer's courses of instruction from Maggie, their meetings usually included acid, hashish, and cocaine.

It was the mid-seventies. For them the war was over, and they were doing their best to join the long hairs in whatever hip revolution might be in vogue at the moment. Eventually they saw less and less of each other. Ron had enrolled in an alternative study program at the University of Hawaii called New College, and Jammer's hours at the Ramparts became more and more like a real job.

Somewhere in New Mexico thirty years later, Windjammer recalled Finch's warning for the second time this evening. He couldn't sleep. There was heat lightning off to the southwest, and outside the tractors sleeping berth the high desert wind was whipping. Finch's words came back to him, "Listen Jammer, if I were you, I'd stay as far away from Loeffler as I possibly could."

Windjammer made no immediate plans either to stay away from Loeffler or to seek him out. But he knew deep down inside that eventually he would need a certain clarification from Loeffler. It didn't make any difference. Loeffler found him again a week later. It was the middle of the week. Jammer had arrived at Ke Nui place around ten p.m. on Wednesday evening with Natalie. They got high with the others at the beach house on the North Shore, and then the entire group of eleven or so all gathered on the lanai overlooking Pupakea beach and the Banzai Pipeline. The whitewater from the surf line was no more than fifty yards away and in the partial moonlight, only part of its sparkling effervesce was evident. Ka'ena Point jutted out into the roaring Pacific nearly fifteen miles to the west, silhouetted by a three quarter moon and medium cloud cover which made it look like a ghostly uninhabited corner of paradise that it was. The talk and anticipation was all about the huge swell that was expected by sunrise. Today's swell had been flawless at ten to twelve feet. But tomorrow promised a twenty foot swell, and at sunup the best surfers in the world would paddle out through the treacherous currents and riptides to breaks like Lani Aekea, Rocky Point, Avalanche, Sunset, Waiamea Bay, and of course the Pipeline, right in front of them.

Windjammer and Natalie had dated on and off for the last six months, and both knew they were each seeing other lovers, but it was no big deal. This evening Natalie also knew Windjammer would not initiate sex. He never did on nights before a big swell. Others did, but not Windjammer. It wasn't as if he were hoarding all of his physical prowess, strength, and stamina for tomorrow's waves. It was more like he was hoarding and protecting his spirit, his spiritual energy, his soul for tomorrow. In fact, that's exactly what he was doing.

Before he and Natalie would lay together in sleep, Windjammer walked the beach alone. He dove into the shore break and swam maybe sixty feet out then fought furiously to escape the dangerous riptide which he knew would almost take him. When delivered back to the beach by a six footer he scrambled up the beach just beyond the receding backwash. He sat and looked back out to mother ocean, now in her darkness, in her secretive state. Her saltiness and organic ooze was still dripping off his skin and he talked with his Hawaiian ocean spirit brothers. "Brothers of the sea, I am with you tonight. I know you want me to come out to the deep places with you tonight, and I marvel at your strength and your joy even on this night before the swell. I will come with you brothers. I will ride with you tomorrow in the early light. We will play together. We will live for the big ones. We will offer ourselves as a pebble of sand for the fury of the moment of truth."

He talked with his brother spirits until the wind dried his skin. Then he returned to the beach house and sought out the best place available for any solitude. He went into the small storage room and lit the candle. All was quite. The entire household had given up on the evenings festivities a half hour ago. He sat with his back straight and his legs overlapping and stared through the candle flame making a chant out of the sound of OMMMMMMMM. Many who practiced transcendental meditation were able to block out all distractions and find an inner sanctum. Windjammer was able to do this and more. He invited his ocean spirit brothers to join him, and they did.

The next morning Windjammer and Natalie walked the half mile or so along the beach towards the east, towards Sunset Beach. The sun, flush in their face, burned the ocean surface it was slowly lumbering out of. But there was a monstrous rippling going on at its base. Long intent lines rolled towards shore at its base. The Sunset break was holding up at twenty-five feet. Windjammer's breakfast of banana's, granola, and papaya rumbled around his stomach for a lap or two, and he was glad he had summoned his ocean spirit brothers to be with him today.

A few minutes later they were at a point where huge lava rock outcroppings jutted out of the violent shore break and white water foam. Windjammer stopped to study the channel which would after a half hour or more lead him out to the line up, a mile or more at sea. Natalie had gone on to the wide crescent shaped beach where girl friends, families, tourist, rescue squads, and cameras would congregate. Before long some of the other women from the beach house would join her there.

Windjammer gazed out to Mother Ocean again, focusing much of his attention on the channel. He saw two heads and shoulders bob into view a quarter mile out, the sun spearing them for only a second, then the swells swallowing them up again. Probably the two were Rabbit, the Hawaiian, and Bruce, the Australian – two that Windjammer figured would be here bright and early. He looked back at the beach he had just come from and there were others coming his way. Their surfboards tucked under an arm, their golden brown skin rippling with muscles only swimmers and surfers possessed – heavy on the lats, the shoulders, triceps, biceps, and pecs. Not so heavy on the legs. Windjammer looked behind him towards the palm trees, checking the wind. It was blowing offshore.

Two others joined him at his vantage point, and after nearly fifteen more minutes of watching and studying the channel, the line up, the wind and Mother Ocean's rhythm, Windjammer dashed to a relatively smooth section of shore break. He threw his nine foot long surfboard down on the backwash and expertly slammed his center of gravity, his belly button, to the exact fulcrum point on the board. He paddled furiously at the water and noticed over his shoulder there were two others behind him.

After ten minutes the rip tide had total control of the three paddlers and had taken them a quarter mile west of where they had started. Their own labor had taken them the same distance from the shoreline. At this crucial location only pure brute strength would be able to get them beyond the rip tide into deeper water where they could finally turn back towards the east, towards the Sunset break. All three were more than up to the challenge. If they had not been up to it, they would have found themselves three miles at sea and some eight miles down the western coastline somewhere in the blue Pacific beyond the channel leading in to Haleiwa Harbor. But they were on the right track now. Windjammer could see Rabbit and Bruce nearly a half mile northeast of him. They were quickly approaching the line up and just to their right there was a fifteen footer on the inside peeling off perfectly with a tube big enough to conceal an automobile without it getting wet.

Then Jammer noticed huge swells a half mile north of Rabbit's and Bruce's position. If they held up they would be swelling up and peaking in about thirty seconds. Did Rabbit and Bruce see them coming? They sure did! Windjammer saw them adjust their course back to the northwest to try and paddle beyond the oncoming mountains of ocean before they were trapped inside, or worse yet, sent tumbling over the falls, backwards. They scratched and clawed at the monstrous wall of water approaching them, their stomachs and guts quivering as if something had sucked all the contents out.

For Rabbit and Bruce their first moment of truth of this still very early morning was only seconds away. Everest has its moments of truth. Two hundred feet above is the summit. Your watch tells you that you are already on the razor's edge – the time up, the time back to this spot, then the time back to the last base camp is running out. It could go either way. Death is as close as your icy breathe in front of your nose.

Motorcycle daredevils have their moment of truth. The instant the tires leave the launch ramp is when you know what's going to happen; not when you approach the landing ramp.

A nineteen year old boy in an exposed rice paddy notices just a hint of movement in the tree line sixty meters away, and he knows what is about to happen. Does he open up or wait for it to happen to him. The moment of truth has arrived. Death is on the doorstep.

Rabbit and Bruce wondered in a micro-instant how they had allowed themselves to be sucked into this bad scene. They knew better, but in their haste to be first out and first to drop in on a twenty-five foot blue-green living wall of water, they had failed to pay Mother Ocean the respect she demands. Now the lip of the first monster wave of the set was being persuaded by the offshore ten knot wind to hold just a few more precious seconds. The thin nearly transparent part of the lip was thirty yards to their right and you could see the sun coming through the windblown spray at the top, and you could also see it was now overcoming the offshore wind and began tumbling towards the bottom. Rabbit and Bruce were half way up the face and had another fifteen feet to get to the top. Now the lip was a few feet directly above them and the thunder of the explosions to their right and behind them spurred them into four, five, six more savage paddle strokes. They broke through the lip at the last second and wasted no time picking up the stroke again. Often the second, third, or fourth wave of a set are the largest. The last few waves will usually be smaller. Then there is the interval between sets. Mother Ocean is quelled for perhaps ten minutes. The surfers can swim after a lost board, or re-think their reasons for being here in the first place. For the surfers who've had good luck and good rides they can groove on Mother Ocean's awesome power and majesty.

Windjammer and the two paddling with him were approaching the line up. After having seen Rabbit and Bruce nearly tumble over the falls on that first set, they allowed plenty of cushion between the break and where they would line up. Still, out here, Mother Ocean always held the hold card. Rabbit caught the first ride of the day, and from the beach a mile away about all you could see was a streaking silver wake cutting top to bottom, right to left across a twenty-three footer that held nicely all the way to the inside reef where Rabbit tore through a perfect twelve foot tube for at least five seconds.

Then Bruce, the Australian, dropped in on a monster that he nearly wiped out on. Once he'd made his turn to the right halfway down the face, he realized the wall in front of him wasn't going to hold up. He cut back hard left and just got proned out on the board in an attempt to play it safe when it seemed to him like half the Pacific Ocean came down on him. He had time to take a deep breathe, wrap his arms under the board and lock on for dear life. Twenty seconds later he and his board bobbled up in front of a gnarly whitewater freeway propelling him in towards the beach. His chin would take fifteen stitches, but he would paddle back out a half hour later.

Windjammer had a terrific morning. His timing was perfect. His judgment and knowledge of what to do at the moment of truth was infallible. By nine a.m. there were over thirty surfers at the Sunset break. Most of the sets had waves between twenty and twenty eight feet. They were getting larger now, but there was a problem. The off shore wind had begun to shift and everyone knew that if the wind direction continued to deteriorate, the break would be impossible to ride in a half hour. Surfers call it 'blown out'.

Most of the thirty were already heading in. They would catch one more on the outside and ride it as far as possible then catch the twelve footers on the inside break and cruise on in towards the beach. Nobody had been hurt bad so far. Other than Bruce's stitches, only some coral cuts, some bruises, and a few teeth knocked out.

Windjammer was on the outside with three others trying to get a feel for the next set they could see rumbling relentlessly towards them. OH MY GOD!! Glory Hallelujah! These were thirty footers coming at them, or bigger! Every one of them!

The crowd on the beach all sensed and saw the drama approaching. Everyone pointed outside – *way outside,* probably two miles from the beach. Without a doubt the largest set of the day. The surf photographers all had their cameras rolling. A murmur started going up and down the beach. Even the cars on Kam Highway behind the beach stopped in the middle of the road to look out to sea.

Richard Loeffler zeroed his field glasses on the four surfers the farthest on the outside and could see they were furiously paddling farther out. They didn't have much of a choice. Nobody wanted to be trapped on the inside of this set. Loeffler saw that two of them were aiming to the west towards maximum safety. But the other two, Windjammer and another haole, Bryant Harrison, were veering somewhat to the east.

Now the whole beach picked up on what was happening. The murmur changed to open shouting and it erupted all along the beach. A young local shouted out the loudest and summed up perfectly what the crowd was witnessing. "Dee two haoles, dey go for dee beeg one on dee outside. OOOOOOHHHH MAN!! Dey neva goin' to make it!!"

But an older Hawaiian who only came to the beach on days like this felt differently. The graying hair, nearly shoulder length, and weathered red-brown skin the texture of a football, concealed a rare spiritual presence that was part of the man. He was a kahuna. He was called on from time to time to perform certain spiritual tasks. Only full blooded Hawaiians or people with mixed Hawaiian blood called on him. He might have been asked to consecrate a location that a family wanted special spiritual favors bestowed on. He might have been asked to be a medium to the spirit world. These were the kinds of things he was asked to do. Although he had never been involved with the young haole surfer named Windjammer, he knew that he should be here for him today.

"It's Jammer and Harrison," shouted one of the men in the crowd Natalie was with. The man had an excellent pair of field glasses and could see in much greater detail the drama that was unfolding. Windjammer had already made up his mind. He was not going to attempt a drop-in on the first wave. He just had a feeling that the second or third in the set would be the biggest wave so far today. Bryant Harrison was a superb athlete but was not even in the same league with Windjammer when it came to wave judgment and that sixth sense of what to do at the moment of truth. For the last half hour he'd been following Windjammer and unsuccessfully attempting to duplicate his every move. Credit was due at least for him knowing his limitations. But now he was following Windjammer to the outside where the third wave in the set would turn out to be a thirty-eight foot killer wave.

At this point Windjammer did not know that Bryant Harrison was close behind him. All of his focus, and then some, was on the monster set barreling down on them. He just cleared the first wave and from it's crest he could see fairly well numbers two and three zeroing in on him. Three was going to be the one, but as the wind direction became more and more on shore, he realized it might not hold. That's when he heard Harrison behind him, "YAHOOOOOEEEEEE!!" Harrison had beat number one crashing and sending him over the falls by a millisecond, and he was verbally letting it all hang out.

OH NO! This guy has been tagging along behind me and now here he is with the biggest wave of the day twenty seconds away. Doesn't he see it may be blown out the rest of the day and the only thing that will save our butt would be a helicopter pick up? But he didn't have time to worry about this young dude. There's an unwritten rule in surfing. The hard lessons you learn on your own. Nobody is expected to bail you out of stupid decisions, even if they might be life threatening. When you paddle out, it's you and Mother Ocean – that's it. The second thing that went through Windjammer's mind was *God I hope he will paddle like a madman back towards the west and try to escape what is now very near – number two and three.*

That second thought lasted a split second, and then everything Windjammer had was now focused on number two. He clawed his way up that mountain of water as if a thousand demons were stabbing at his surfboard with their honed pitchforks. He made it. Then he laid his eyes on a sight that very few men on planet Earth will ever see. A wave so awesome, so powerful, so ruthless, he thought his heart would jump out of his chest. Other men might see it in surf flicks or on TV, but they would not see it, feel it, as Windjammer would. At this very moment he was about to become part of it. 'Become one with it' wouldn't be correct. You might become one with a six footer, or a ten footer, or even a fifteen foot wave, but you don't become one with a thirty-eight foot wave. For a moment you become part of it, and if you survive, you will have been akin to it. But if you become 'one with it' you would have vanished into wet star dust as the wave itself would surely do in just a few moments.

Jammer raced to the spot he felt was perfect for the drop in. On a wave this size there would not be an inch to miscalculate. Years later, most surfers attempting to ride a wave this size would be towed down the face by a jet ski in order to get the speed necessary. But not Jammer, not today. He was nearing the spot. The wave was cresting, the windblown lip trailing thirty feet above as if in a hurricane, and now the moment of truth. Windjammer acted unconsciously. He swung his board instantly towards the beach and flailed at the water for all the speed he could generate. Again, his timing was perfect, but still the speed alone would not get the board sliding downward. The lip of the wave, now being buffeted by not the off shore winds but the on shore wind, smacked the tail of his board, violently lifting it for a split second. The nose dropped and down the wave he started. The blast of salty wind-whipped spray blinded Windjammer as he instantly came to his feet. He was unable to see Harrison still struggling up the face trying valiantly not to get sucked back over the falls.

Windjammer's board plummeted down and instinctively he leaned into the wall of water to his right to begin the turn and try to outrace the mountain of water closing in on him. His eyes were still burning, but at least now he could see. Everything he saw he saw in a blur but with perfect clarity at the same time. The distress signal arrived at his brain: HARRISON IS DEAD AHEAD! There won't be time to bail out. You are going to hit him.

The old Hawaiian Kahuna on the beach heard the gasps and shouts from the throngs of onlookers, but he was already well into a deep chant in the old Hawaiian language that no one else could understand. Translated, it said, "We go to the waves, we swim with the sharks, we fish for to eat, the sun shares the sea, we come to be with the sun and the sea. We come in our canoes. We come on our boards. We come and swim like the fish. Take us close to you spirits of the sea, spirits of the waves, spirits of the sharks. We are your brothers. We come not from the land. We come from you. You are our brothers. We live with you in the sea with the sun. We are your brothers. Protect us. We are your brothers, protect us."

Windjammer cut back hard left in a futile attempt to miss Bryant Harrison, but the 10 inch skeg on his board caught the tail of Harrison's board solid. Windjammer was racing down the blue mountain of water at nearly 45 m.p.h., so there was no doubt about what the outcome of this collision was going to be. The only question was, would there be any survivors?

* * *

Chapter Eight

The citizens of the United States had for the first time since World War II put away their petty political bickering and pulled together to deal with the aftermath of the 9–11 attacks. It wouldn't last long, but for a few months, it seemed most Americans agreed with President Bush's insertion of American troops into Afghanistan and other steps the administration was taking. Certainly Toby Etheridge was pro war on terrorism. He simply could not understand why any American would not support any and all measures to rid the earth of fanatical Islamic terrorists.

Thanksgiving came, then Christmas. Toby had been able to get home for a few days. His big truck, a 2000 model Freightliner Deluxe was parked down by the barn on an eighty foot long section of gravel he had dumped, graded, and packed for that very purpose. With a fifty-three-foot semi-trailer hooked to his Freightliner tractor there was no room to spare on the gravel parking pad.

On Christmas Eve he had been in New York City, but because he was bound and determined to be home for Christmas, he drove straight through the night pulling in his driveway about 4:00 a.m. He sure was not going to miss Christmas at home in this, only the latter part of his second month as an over-the-road truck driver. He was learning quickly to keep one set of log books for the DOT cops and another set of log books for his company's safety department. If they caught him driving over ten hours straight, it would have cost him a significant fine.

After he had parked the rig on the pad he grabbed his shaving kit, dirty laundry bag and prepared to climb down out of the cab. He noticed the paperback novel he had been reading over two months ago back in Memphis at the Mountaintop Transport training facility. It had been lying in the corner behind the dirty laundry bag. 'I wonder if Windjammer made it back to the beach alive,' he thought. Once he had started driving, Toby's hectic schedule had stolen any free time he might have had for reading. But that image of two surfers crashing on the face of a thirty something foot wave was an image he still thought about. Oh well, Windjammer will just have to wait a little longer. Nothing is going to rob me from time with Sarah and the kids.

Four hours later, he felt Sarah moving under the covers next to him. They both heard voices in the living room and knew that Carolyn and Derrick couldn't contain the Christmas morning anticipation any longer and were sorting through some of the still unopened gift boxes under the tree. Toby rolled toward Sarah and wrapped her up in his arms. "I wish I had you like this in my sleeper cab a couple of nights ago." He nibbled on the back of her neck and ear and continued. "But since I didn't, I guess that other girl wasn't too bad."

Sarah laughed, "The way that truck smells, I can't imagine what kind of other girl would climb in there with you."

"Well I'll tell you what kind. The kind that appreciates a real man, a man that could give her what she wants, what she needs," with heavy emphasis on the needs, and he snuggled up a little closer to her.

She laughed again, "What you need mister truck driver is going to have to wait. Come on, the kids are waiting."

Later, over their traditional Christmas morning breakfast of country ham, scrambled eggs, biscuits, and potato cakes with sour cream, Toby was telling every one about his travels. He had already been in thirty-five states. He really seemed to be enjoying it, but certainly some of the things that happened gave Sarah cause for real concern. As for Derrick and Carolyn, they were immune to all the false bravado, all the macho man bull crap their dad had been spewing for years. Usually they got the Alabama football routine: how great the Crimson Tide was and had been; the twelve national titles; the greatest coach of all time, Bear Bryant; on and on; a never ending stream of crap, in their opinion. When it wasn't Alabama football, it was Toby's right wing political views. Carolyn and Derrick cringed anytime someone or something would get him started. He had, in their opinion, no ability to be open minded or fair. Everything was black or white to their dad. Sometimes he would make an attempt to have a real conversation with them and listen to their side of an issue and really try to allow his thick skull to actually consider a point of view that wasn't pro war, pro life, republican, pro God in schools, pro America as top dog on the world scene, but it never worked out. It always ended in his sermonizing about right and wrong, good and evil, American values always supreme, and particularly since 9-11, his tirades, 'that it's time we did something'. Derrick and Carolyn loved their dad, but they would prefer he be a lot less vocal about all the macho posturing. Now that he was a truck driver, they feared they would be getting more of the same when he came home, only now it would be about 18 wheelers.

Sure enough, after all the gifts had been opened, breakfast finished, and a football game or two, Toby insisted they all go out to take a tour of the inside of his truck. He proudly explained what each gauge and each switch was, its function, and when and how to use it. He explained the air brake system and the difference between the service brake, the hand brake, and the parking brakes; one for the tractor and one for the trailer. Then he went into all the communications and entertainment on board: the CB radio, satellite radio, A.M.-F.M. radio and CD player, the qual-com satellite computer system, then his own wireless laptop satellite system, and finally the TV perched on a shelf between the front seats and the sleeper birth in the rear. He ended the tour by showing the storage area under the bottom bunk, the small refrigerator, and an explanation of the heating and cooling system which was electronically controlled and would even start and stop the trucks engine for power when the truck was not rolling and he was sleeping.

They were duly impressed. Even Derrick felt a little different about his dad's new occupation after the tour of the truck. Before, he wasn't at all sure about the impression his dad's new gig would have on his friends at school. Now he didn't care. He could see his dad was happier than he'd been in years and that he had taken on this new job with a purpose he'd not shown while working at the golf course. It was as if the truck driving was a way to achieve a higher purpose. It was, but none of them knew what it was. Toby barely knew it himself. He only knew he had to continue planning for the execution of the fourth decision. He couldn't believe that already, after less than four months since the 9-11 attacks, the country was showing signs of weakness in its resolve to respond. Thank God for President Bush and Mayor Giuliani, he thought! Without their leadership, where would we be? The democrats were already faltering, egged on by the left wing media. But while some were already drifting from what Toby knew had to be done, Toby wasn't. He was beginning to see the structure of his fourth decision starting to take shape. Yes, the truck driving part of it was coming along nicely - not easily, but it was coming along none-the-less.

The break-in period with his driver trainer had offered few surprises that he hadn't anticipated, except for one. Although he and the fifty other trainees, had been warned during the two week crash course that Mountaintop Transport had put them through, until he had actually been assigned an experienced driver trainer that he would team-drive with, he'd had no way of knowing what extreme sleep deprivation could do to a person. Even back in his Navy days he had not been subjected to extended periods of sleep loss that he was getting in this truck driving business.

It was seven weeks ago, on his first trip out with Dave Nelson, his trainer, that the reality of serious over-the-road truck driving sank in on him. From the beginning Dave was no-nonsense. They started from Memphis late in the afternoon. Dave drove the first seventy-five miles, north, up I-55 across the Missouri state line and pulled into the rest area. His only sign of interest in Toby at all were questions he asked him about past truck driving experience. Toby had none. There was no need to find out any personal information. Dave had learned, many times over, that the less you knew about a trainee's background, the better. Many of the new drivers were young, and many had a trail of trouble with the law. His final judgment on Toby Etheridge would only be made after the four week training period. The obvious was already a feather in Toby's cap as far as Dave was concerned – his age. Unlike the really young trainees, Dave sensed that Toby had a healthy dose of self confidence and of course, maturity that only fifty years could give a man. Still, it remained to be seen what kind of a driver Toby would make. It was time to find out.

"After a pee break, I'll ride shotgun, and you'll drive us into St. Louis," and Dave carefully lowered his four-hundred pounds down the two safety steps on the driver's side and waddled off towards the men's room. When they were both ready to go Toby adjusted the drivers seat and steering wheel to his six foot four inch frame. He scanned all the gauges with special attention to the two air pressure gauges. He used the switch on the dash to adjust the mirrors to where he could just see only the very tail end of the fifty-three foot trailer he was pulling. Then he snapped in his seat belt strap and was working the clutch and the gear shift through the ten speed gear box hoping he wouldn't miss a gear when he pulled out in a few seconds. Dave was looking a little impatient, but said nothing. Finally Toby pushed in the yellow and red air brake release valves, put it in third gear, and was for the first time in his life pulling a load of some forty three thousand pounds headed for Kansas City, via St. Louis. Toby's progression through the remaining seven gears left a lot to be desired, but Dave had seen worse. After reaching cruising speed of 68 mph and settling in the right hand or 'granny lane', Toby was feeling good and, for the moment, had almost forgotten the unfinished plans he had been forming up in his mind for the fourth decision. He put the truck on cruise control, took his foot off the accelerator, and savored a feeling of satisfaction. He was progressing slowly and deliberately towards what he knew he must do.

Dave kept a pretty close eye on Toby's driving for the first two hundred miles. Then, and only when he was confident that Toby had enough skill not to kill both of them, he stuffed his four-hundred pounds back in the sleeper and stretched out on the lower bunk. "Toby, you look like you're doing okay. Wake me up when we get close to Kansas City. I'll direct you into the terminal. Then we'll fuel up, drop this load, pick up the next load, and head on down towards Austin."

Toby was happy to continue driving. This wasn't anything at all like the two week crash course at the Mountaintop Transport training facility in Memphis. There, he was lucky to get a one hour stretch of straight highway driving time. Most of their time was spent on practicing their backing skills. The old saying was, 'Anybody can drive an eighteen wheeler straight down the road. It's putting one on a loading dock at three in the morning, in the pouring rain, with two inches to spare on either side that separates a truck driver from a wannabe.' *How true that old saying was!* Toby thought to himself. Was he happy to continue driving? Absolutely yes. Was he confident that he was wide awake enough to do so? No. *I'm sure Dave will take over when we get to Kansas City. That lower bunk is going to feel good when I hit it.*

By two a.m. Toby had topped off both fuel tanks, dropped the first trailer, and picked up the next loaded trailer. Dispatch said this one had to be in Austin, Texas by six a.m. the next morning. All of the communications from dispatch came through the qual-com computer, and Toby was starting to see that learning it would take more than a little effort. More important at this moment, Toby was really worried that Dave had forgotten that a human being had to sleep. However, he wasn't about to bring it up. He could sense that Dave did things Dave's way. Dave was *the man* in this situation, and to start whining about sleep would only identify himself as a wimp – not a truck driver at all. Toby sure wasn't going to do that.

They pulled out of K.C. around two thirty a.m. Toby was driving southwest on I-35, and Dave was snoring in the bottom bunk, his rolls of flab flopping about on his deeply buried skeletal frame like Jell-O with every bump in the road. Approaching Wichita, Kansas, Toby was fighting to stay awake. The techniques they had mentioned in driving school were not working. He had kept the windows open until he could stand the cold no longer. He stuck his head out to get the full blast of the icy wind. He turned the radio up loud. Screw Dave, he thought. It probably won't faze him. Nothing seemed to work. Toby was still nodding off, and worse, he sensed a panic attack coming on. Finally, he resorted to physical activity. He shook his hands, fingers, arms, one at a time while the other remained on the wheel. Then he rotated his head, neck, and torso in both directions. He stood up as much as possible while keeping his head low enough to still see the road. If he slowed down or stopped these gyrations he would immediately drop off again. After this happened three times, he realized he couldn't keep this up much longer. Toby abandoned his plans of staying off coffee and pulled over at the next truck stop. He had been on a health kick prior to the two week crash course because he had felt it was necessary to slim down and get in as good of shape as possible. The plans he'd been forming on the fourth decision might require some physical exertion. So far he had been successful at dropping twenty pounds down to two-twenty, but this morning was no time to hang on to the coffee cessation. The hot java felt good and tasted good going down. He was back behind the wheel, still fighting it, but not nodding off like he had been.

Finally, as if an unheard alarm had gone off, Dave was shifting around in the bunk and wrestling his enormous body up to a sitting position. "It's my turn. Pull over."

It was six thirty a.m., the Kansas prairie already had shafts of pinks, purples, and crimson working their way through the gray cloud bank to the east. Toby spotted an exit ramp a mile away, pulled the rig over, and they traded places. He was asleep instantly, but it was a fitful experience at best. It would be weeks before he adjusted to the routine of team driving, and also before he discovered that Dave himself was not in a state of hibernation for ten hours at a time when he was in the sleeper. Toby would come to learn that Dave was a very light sleeper; he was in fact very aware of most everything that was going on when Toby was driving.

The tour of Toby's truck completed, the four of them walked back to the house. The December wind was nipping at them, and the winter sunset was an hour away.

"Mom tells me you're not going to stay on the golf team," Toby's arm was around Carolyn's back, and his hand was on her shoulder.

Oh no, Carolyn thought. *This is the first time he's asked anything about it. I better be careful.* "I've kind of been thinking about spending more time with the forensics team and the drama club. It's hard to, you know, keep all three going at the same time." She hoped that would suffice, but continued, "We are starting work on the spring play when we go back next week. Daddy, do you think you can be home for it? I'm going to try for a lead role." She stopped walking and turned to face him, her pretty eyes full of pleading and anticipation. She had expertly shifted the subject away from golf and the horrible memories there-in, the one secret Toby could never find out. It worked.

Now on the defensive, he replied, "Sure Darlin'. You know I wouldn't miss that for anything."

Later that night Toby was rubbing Sarah's feet. Derrick had gone out and Carolyn was at a friend's house two farms away. Toby was sprawled back over the bed with only his shorts on, three pillows under his head and shoulders, Sarah's legs on his chest and her left foot in his hand. They spent many hours rubbing each other's feet. It had been a practice of theirs going all the way back to their dating days.

"Hey, did I hear something from Carolyn today that doesn't quite fit? I don't know what it is. There's just something about quitting the golf team. I can't put my finger on it." He dropped her left foot and started working on the right one.

"No honey, I don't think so," she lied. Sarah never did totally accept Carolyn's explanation for the bump and bruise on her cheekbone. Not that it could not have happened at a pick-up co-ed soccer game where one of the boys had accidentally run over her. It certainly could have. Whatever the real cause of the minor injury, she never did feel it was important enough to badger her daughter about it. On the other hand something just wasn't right, and it could have had something to do with leaving the golf team. But whatever it was, it certainly wasn't anything worth getting Toby's antennae up about. "I think she's got some friends in drama and forensics she's wanted to spend more time with. There's no other reason I know of."

That satisfied Toby. He knew that Sarah would have known if there were any problems with Carolyn. Like most mothers, Sarah's motherly instincts and intuitions were sharply honed.

"Good, I was a little worried. I just wasn't sure." He stopped working on her right foot and started rubbing a little higher on Sarah's legs. The kids were both gone.

Later, on Christmas night, Toby and Sarah were in the living room snuggled up together on the sofa under a blanket enjoying the heat from the woodstove and the twinkling lights on the Christmas tree. They heard Derrick come in the back door and make his way to the kitchen. He showed up a few minutes later in the living room with some left over turkey, dressing, gravy, and a coke.

"Is that for me?" Toby asked.

"You wish, old man."

They bantered back and forth like this most of the time. Sarah thought that one day they might go a little too far. She didn't want to think about what might happen then. If it ever did go too far, Derrick was very capable of holding his own against Toby. He was stronger and nearly as big.

"So tell me old man, have you had any real adventures out there on the road yet?" Derrick had to admit he was getting more and more interested in this new truck driving phase of his dad's life.

Toby wasn't sure if Derrick was sincere, and of course there was nothing he could tell him about *why* he became a truck driver, but as for the adventure, well yes, there was plenty to tell – at least coming from *his* perspective. After all, there was a vast difference between driving twelve miles to the golf course, supervising a crew, then returning home at night, and pulling seventy five thousand pounds of steel and freight down the road. There was nothing he knew of that could duplicate or exceed the rush he got every time he started out on a new trip. No driver, experienced or not, could anticipate what was going to happen when you aimed your load at California, or Canada, or Maine. You might try your best to get it there in three or four days without hurting anyone, but of course, things don't always go smoothly. Toby said, "Well, I'm not sure whether you'd call it adventure or not, but I've been scared as hell a couple of times."

"What happened?" Derrick leaned forward, convincing Toby he was interested.

"Well, after my four weeks with Dave, they had me team driving with another rookie for a couple of weeks."

"I'll bet he won't forget that experience! How could another human being live that close to you for two weeks?" Sarah, like Derrick, wasn't hesitant to poke fun at Toby. It took more than good natured joking to bring out his darker side.

"It was supposed to have been four weeks, but he quit on me. I don't know what happened to him, if he continued his training, or left the company."

"Why did he quit?" Derrick asked.

"I'm not sure he did, but if he did, I think it had something to do with the night we were coming out of Denver. We were westbound on I-70 going up into the mountains. L.B. was driving. I was back in the lower bunk sleeping."

"L.B.?" Derrick asked.

"Yeah, L.B. That's what we called him. He was a young black kid from Mississippi. We got along alright I guess. The first two weeks we had been on a trip to Texas, then back to the East Coast, then down to South Carolina and Georgia. I came home for a couple of days, then we got a load all the way to Salt Lake City, so we were in Denver that night. We had just fueled up at the company terminal. I crawled in the back and went to sleep. I guess I had been sleeping for two hours. When I woke up almost rolling out of the bunk, the truck was going down a pretty good grade. Then I realized I smelled something unusual, you know, something I shouldn't have smelled. I asked L. B. if he smelled anything out of the ordinary. He said he did. Then it dawned on me. I asked him if he'd been riding the brakes hard? I knew we had been coming downhill, and I knew we had on around forty thousand pounds of freight. He said, 'Yeah, I had to.' I was wide awake then. I asked him how long he'd been on the brakes, and he said 'At least an hour'. I was more wide awake, now."

Derrick interrupted, "What's the big deal? Aren't you supposed to use your brakes coming downhill?"

"Well sure, but not continuously for an hour. That will burn them up."

"What do you do?"

"You use your transmission. You downshift until you can reduce your speed – enough so you don't have to sit on your brakes."

"So L. B. had not been downshifting?"

Toby turned his head a little and squinted his eyes a bit, "Not enough. otherwise, he wouldn't have had to sit on his brakes the way he was. Anyway, that's what we smelled – the brake linings heating up."

"So, what happened?"

"Well, I suggested we pull over and let them cool off. I guess L. B. was getting a little touchy about the situation, but he did pull over. I moved up in the shotgun seat, and as I did I could see it was snowing like crazy outside. I asked L. B. how long it had been snowing, and he said ever since we left Denver. I could see there was at least four or five inches on the ground."

Derrick was now beginning to place all these images into his internal movie projector, and a scratchy black and white flickering visualization played on the screen in his head – two rookie truck drivers, one old and white, the other, young and black, trying to hold back forty thousand pounds of freight, coming down the backside of the Rocky Mountains in a blinding snowstorm at one in the morning. *HMMM,* he thought, *this is getting more interesting all the time.* "What happened then?"

"We sat there a minute. I was looking out the window on my side and noticed a sign that said RUNAWAY TRUCK RAMP. In the dark and the falling snow, I could just make out the upward incline of the emergency off ramp. I don't guess L. B. saw it when he pulled over, but he had stopped directly in front of it!"

"So, what's the big deal?"

"Nothing except, what if another truck coming down the mountain behind us needed it? We had it blocked off. I told L. B. in no uncertain terms he had to move it, and I guess I came across bossy because he said, 'The hell I am. I ain't driving one more inch.' He got up out of the seat, went back in the sleeper, closed the curtain to the cab, and didn't say another word to me for twenty-four hours."

"What did he do, flip out?"

"That's the way I figured it." Toby got up, went to the kitchen for another cup of coffee. When he got back, Derrick was still there, obviously waiting for the rest of the story.

"He just quit driving?"

"Like I said, for at least twenty-four hours he did." Toby sat back down next to Sarah who was dozing on and off.

"What did you do?" Derrick asked impatiently.

Kids! Toby thought. *This morning Derrick could have cared less. Now he wants all the details yesterday. If only he knew. If only he knew what it is really like. What it is really like to be barreling down I-25 a hundred miles south of Colorado Springs, trying to make New Mexico by sun-up. The loneliness, the sweet loneliness. You, the open road, the vast, windswept plains. A man can think. If only he knew, but then if he did, he might get this same love-hate for it I'm getting. Actually, it's more of...should I even say it? It's more love than hate. What am I becoming? A real truck driver? That's not why I got into it, but maybe that's where it's going.*

"What could I do? We had to get off that entrance to the runaway ramp, and we had to get it down the mountain. It wasn't my turn to drive, but L. B. wasn't going to. The first thing I did was ease it on down the shoulder out of the way of the runaway truck ramp. Then I got on the CB and got a comeback from another driver. I told him he was talking to a brand new, greener than green, rookie driver, and I wasn't sure how to get this load down the mountain safely. You know, I was worried our brakes might burn up, and the weight of our load, and the snow and ice on the road. I didn't tell him I was scared as hell and was afraid of sliding right over the edge of the mountain, but I was."

"What did he say?"

"He was very helpful. I guess he'd been there before. He took it real slow and explained a few things to me that weren't covered in my two week driving school. The main thing, he said, was don't worry too much about burning up the brakes. He said to look at the type of snow we're getting tonight. It's not the real dry, light stuff. It's wet and slushy. He said it will actually cool your brakes off. I asked him about using my "Jake Brake" that the training book says not to use it in wet or snowy conditions. He said most of the experienced drivers will use it on a night like this but not on packed ice. Finally, I asked him what gear I should be in to hold the load back? He said whatever gear you are most comfortable with; just shift down as low as you want and crawl down the mountain if it makes you feel safe. Now *that* really made sense to me! That's exactly what I did."

"How long did it take you?"

"Oh, probably less than two hours, and I was really coming down slow. It's one of those things, that until you actually do it, it's hard to explain the feeling of what it's really like. For a while I felt we might and probably would, slide off the mountain at any time."

"Wow! Some night, huh?" Derrick still wanted the lowdown on L.B. "What happened to L. B.?"

"You know, it's the craziest thing, but I believe that night might have ruined him as a driver. Somewhere around 4:30 in the morning, after we were down, out of the snow, on dry road, I stopped at a truck stop to get some breakfast. I said, 'L. B., come on, let's go in and get some breakfast. It's on me. Let's just put this night behind us and forget it.' He didn't say a word, and he didn't come in with me. I drove on into Salt Lake City later that day; we dropped the load and picked up another one going straight back to Denver. Of course, by this time I was driving illegal. I was out of my allotted ten driving hours for a twenty-four hour period, and out of my seventy allotted hours for an eight day period. So, he was driving on the way back to Denver, and he still had not said a word to me. Because of the snow on 70, we took 80 back and finally that night when he pulled over, it all started coming out. I was a honky cracker, and he let me know it, over and over again. I said, 'I don't know what's happened to you, but I do know that you and I are not going to finish this trip together.' He acted shocked but kept up the racial crap. I let him run his mouth with the most vile, obscene racial crap you've ever heard, but I anticipated a fight at any moment."

"Did you all get into it?"

"No, but I thought we would. I got on the qual-com and told Denver dispatch, 'One of the two drivers on board this truck is going to have to be removed.' I told them I didn't care if it was me or him, but before this truck was going to move another inch, one of us was not going to be on it."

"What did they do?"

"They sent out the assistant terminal manager from Denver. We sat there four hours. When he got there, he told L. B. to pack his things up and climb down out of the truck. He took him back to Denver where presumably he was assigned to another driver on another truck."

Derrick pondered all the implications his eighteen year old mind could come up with and settled on the obvious, "When you said you thought it might have ruined him as a driver, what exactly did you mean?"

"I think it's possible his confidence was destroyed. I sure hope not. You know, I thought, at least up until that night, that L. B. was a good kid. I trusted him. All that racial crap coming out really floored me. I have prayed for him since then. I just hope everything worked out for him."

The real cause for the 'racial crap', Toby left unsaid. They had started out, just like Toby had told Derrick, 'getting along all right.' Little did Toby know that L. B. must have hated his cracker attitude from the start: Toby's 'I'll take charge' self confidence, his built-in gene pool of manifest destiny, his reliance on his education, his contacts with successful people.

In the end L.B. had let him have it with both barrels. "Hell! I'd like to see you with your 'better than anybody else, Whitey' attitude, down in the hood. Your ass would get blowed away real quick. That wouldn't go very far when your kids aint' et nuthin' in two days and when your ol' lady's doin' tricks to score some crack. Aint' no Whitey gonna' tell me what to do! And what you pulled on me back in Memphis? That playing of Muddy Waters tapes and axin' me if I like the blues too? Who do you think you are, Honkey? You don't know nuthin' bout' no blues."

It was only days after the incident that Toby felt he could really understand what had happened to L. B. As Toby saw it, L. B. came from a world so different from his own, that it was probably inevitable that a blow-up between the two would have occurred. Toby could see that L. B. was one angry young man. There had been signs of it all along, but Toby had pushed them all aside. There was no need to have gotten into it. What purpose would it have served? Toby's main purpose in the truck driving gig was to get qualified to operate a big truck so he could carry out his fourth decision. He didn't need to get bogged down in some theoretical college class sociological thesis on why some young blacks hate crackers. All he had wanted to do was complete his mandatory four week team driving assignment with another rookie driver. Then he would be qualified to solo drive. The fact that his first assignment had been with a young black hadn't bothered Toby at all. He could have opted out when they met. Either one of them could have declined their joint assignment and been placed with another driver, but they didn't.

Chapter Nine

It was December 27, 2001. Toby would have to go back on the road later that afternoon. He was dispatched to pick up a load of auto parts near Birmingham and take them to a distribution center in Syracuse, New York. Toby knew what this meant – that anytime you get that close to New York City, you were going to have to go into the city – the very thing all rookie drivers hated doing. There were plenty of horror stories floating around about the kind of trouble drivers, especially rookie drivers, could get into in the big east coast cities like New York, Boston, and Philadelphia. Before he left, he wanted to find Coon Dog. There were several questions he needed to ask him.

Toby found him in a work shed behind his cabin. He was curing hams from hogs he had killed yesterday. He was rubbing them down with salt and seasoning, getting ready to hang them up in the smokehouse. Coon Dog saw him coming into the shed, "Well, well, the newest gear jammer in the county."

"You got the jamming part right. But at least I haven't killed anybody yet."

"Here, have a shot." Coon Dog placed a half empty bottle of Jim Beam on the table in front of Toby. He wiped his hands on a towel and rolled a cigarette.

"No thanks, I've got to get on the road as soon as I leave here. I came by to get your thinking on something."

"Sure, whatcha' got?" Coon Dog turned the volume down on Hank Williams on the radio.

"Some drivers and me have been talking about forming up a highway watch group. The idea would be that if we get enough drivers involved, we could be a real force in watching out for suspicious activity out on the highways. If a terrorist were going to use a truck to blow something up, maybe we could stop him."

Coon Dog took a pull on the Jim Beam. "Sounds good so far. What do you need my thinking on?"

"I know a little about the work you did in the Seals, but I don't know the extent of your knowledge about explosives. There are a few things I think would be helpful if you could give me a little insight."

"What kind of things?" If it were anyone other than Toby asking, the conversation would probably be over, but Toby was one of the few that Coon Dog would ever trust. All those nights Toby stayed with him on the phone, the nights that Coon Dog's pain was so unbearable he needed a human voice he could hear, he needed a human ear to listen to him. All those nights, Toby was there for him.

Toby wanted to be very careful about how to proceed. It looked like Coon Dog bit on the lie about the highway watch group. Maybe if he continued on this same track, he could get the information he needed. "You remember the Oklahoma City bombing? Well, I've been thinking. What would prevent a terrorist from doing the exact same thing on another target? What would prevent him from using a truck, or several trucks, with enough explosives in them from blowing up a target as large as and important as the Twin Towers?"

"Nothing, if you didn't know they were coming, or if you hadn't barricaded it off beforehand."

"Exactly! We can't barricade the whole country can we? So, the best way to prevent such an attack would be intelligence. Would you agree? Knowing about the attack before it happens so we had time to stop it."

"Sure that makes sense, but what does that have to do with a highway watch group?" Coon Dog took another pull from the Beam.

"One of the guys in our group is a computer hot shot. He thinks he could come up with a system, a program I guess, that would monitor all sales of the kinds of materials needed to build a bomb like the one McVey used at Oklahoma City. His thinking is that by monitoring all of that kind of information, large transactions of the raw materials for the explosives would be a red flag which would trigger us to notify the government."

"Hell, Toby, the government is already doing it!"

"You think so?" Toby was doing his best to sound surprised and be the totally unaware Joe public citizen.

Coon Dog knew better, but played along, "Hell yes! Of course they are. They've been doing it since maybe even before Oklahoma City. They evidently ain't doing such a fine job of it, but they are doing it."

"You really think so?" Toby stayed with the imbecile role.

"Sure, of course I do." Coon Dog was getting tired of the game, and Toby was aware of it.

"Just for my own curiosity's sake, don't you think a terrorist could get around the government surveillance if he really wanted to? I mean, that he could still get his hands on enough materials to build a large truck bomb, despite what the government is doing to prevent it?"

"I just told you I think the government ain't doing such a good job. Sure a terrorist could get his hands on enough materials to build damn near anything he wanted."

"How?" Toby asked, and Coon Dog told him. Not only how, but what materials were needed and what to do with them.

Toby's trip sheet was filled out. It was his written trip itinerary: the shipper, the consignee, trailer number, bill of lading number, pick-up number, seal number, directions to the shipper and consignee, pick up and delivery appointment times, and anything else he might need to know about the load he was pulling. It was all on his trip sheet. The small refrigerator was packed with sandwich meat, cheese, salad makings, milk, and juice. The dry storage area was filled with cereal, sardines, bread, crackers, cookies, peanut butter, and fruit. His twin one hundred-fifty gallon fuel tanks were topped off, and he had completed his walk around pre-trip inspection of all seventy-two feet of his rig. He thumped all eighteen tires with a ball peen hammer and was satisfied with the sharp T H W A A P ! each tire echoed back. He checked the tractor's fifth wheel grip on the trailer's king pin and the locking arm's handle position which was in. He checked all his lights, mirror adjustments, the glad hands from the tractor to the trailer, the pigtail, and finally he made sure the trailers dollies were up all the way.

He had said his good byes to Sarah, Carolyn, and Derrick early that morning. He was about ready to pull the rig out from the pad near the barn and get the three week trip under way, but there was one more thing he had to do. Before he forgot any details, he wrote down word for word everything Coon Dog had told him about making an ammonia nitrate and fuel oil, truck bomb and placed his notes in the small briefcase he kept his growing file of information in.

He made the hour and a half drive to Birmingham with his mind racing over the information from Coon Dog and was thinking how this new information might mesh with his list of possibilities he'd been compiling for his fourth decision. The more he worked on his plans, and the more he learned about big rig truck driving, the more determined he became. He watched the news and was glad that Bush had gone into Afghanistan, but there was so much more we should be doing he thought here in the homeland. 'By God! I'm going to get to doing it!'

Toby was doing a good job of not alerting anyone around him what he was actually up to. Only Coon Dog had any suspicions, but they were not strong ones. Even if Coon Dog had known the direction of Toby's secret compulsion, he probably would have supported him. On the other hand, if Coon Dog had known the depth of Toby's hatred for Al-Qaeda, he may not have gone along with him. Too many times Coon Dog had seen the death of good men, fanatical patriots who were self proclaimed experts on the difference between good and evil. The survivors were the cooler heads. Toby hid it well, but a cooler head he was not.

He wheeled the big Freightliner through the gate at the security guard shack at the entrance to the shipper where he would back his empty trailer up against a loading dock and wait for probably an hour until he was loaded and could finally start rolling north towards Syracuse. As usual, he realized that the row of some fifteen or twenty gnarly, wizened, old truckers who were already backed in and relaxing in their cabs would be watching him.

Could they tell he was a rookie driver? Even though he was confident about his backing skills, he was never-the-less a little nervous when he had to back the rig into a tight hole. The answer was yes. There were a thousand ways they knew: by the speed he moved through the yard, by his use or non-use of his four way flashers, by the way he got down out of his truck. They knew by the way he used his mirrors, by the clutter or lack of clutter in his cab, by the swing he made on turns, by his braking, by his shifting, and simply, by the way he sized things up that were going on around him. This, in fact, was probably one of the most important ways they knew he was a rookie. To Toby's credit, he was pretty good at sizing up situations going on around him. And his age and life experience bode well for him.

Toby felt the presence of those eyes. To experienced truckers, rookies were trouble. One mistake could get people killed. On the open road rookies were avoided like the plague. In truck yards and on loading docks you couldn't avoid them, but if you could, you would.

Toby went in the shipping office, got his dock assignment, climbed back up in the cab, and then maneuvered his truck into the 'set-up' position – angled at forty-five degrees to the loading dock. He opened both windows to eliminate glare and any false reflections, then cut the steering wheel right in order to push the trailer back in to the left towards the dock. "Oh no!" he shouted to himself. The door number was missing from the empty dock space he was aiming the trailer at. Not being a hundred percent certain he was at the correct dock caused him to hesitate and jerk the truck backwards. *I'm sure those eyes picked that up,* he thought. Then he noticed three dock workers snickering and farting around up on the dock. They were probably betting on how many pull-ups Toby would need to get the trailer into the hole perfectly straight.

Forget them, Toby thought, and he fine tuned his concentration to the task at hand. That was one thing he was very good at doing - blocking out distractions and really focusing on the problem in front of him. After only one pull-up he had the truck straight in the hole and only fifteen feet from the loading dock. He climbed down and went back to open the trailer doors, one more thing that set him apart as a rookie. Experienced drivers opened their trailer doors before they backed a truck to a dock. Toby was aware of this fact but felt he had better vision to see the dock with the doors closed. He was right of course. Many times just the extra two or three inches of unimpaired vision on each side would be the difference in hitting the dock successfully without many pull-ups. What he would soon learn, however, was that not opening the doors first could create a much greater problem.

In less than an hour Toby's trailer was loaded with auto parts. He signed the paperwork that made the load 'his'. That is, he owned forty-two thousand pounds of auto parts until he delivered them in Syracuse and someone on that end signed for them. Hammer down, rolling northeast on Interstate-59 towards Chattanooga, Toby was loosing his busy thinking – the sorting and planning of the information he had been accumulating about the fourth decision. He was replacing those thoughts with the age old, soothing, open road thinking of all truck drivers – where would the next stop be made for coffee or a hot meal; where would he stop to sleep for the night; what was the weather forecast for the next 24 hours; would some sexy seat covers cruise by his always roaming eyes; would anything interesting come across the CB?

Another form of the open road thinking was what Toby called free thinking – letting your mind wander from one thing to another, completely without restraints of any kind – time, place, accuracy...anything. There was also the ability to think deliberately about a very specific item. Whatever it might be, you could dissect it from every conceivable angle. You could think it through and through. You could think it into the ground, and Toby often did. You could do that out on the open road. You had time to do it.

It was this deliberate thinking that Toby was shifting into this time. He'd been out for over three hours now, Chattanooga was behind him, the sad winter sun drowned by fog and gray-black night an hour ago. He'd tired of listening to right-wing talk radio and all the talk of whether Bush was going to force Saddam Hussein's hand on the possession of WMD'S. *Force his hand?* Toby thought. *How about blowing his head off and all the other Arab terrorists?* He was aware of his very un-Christian feelings, but wasn't able to stop himself. He played out several scenarios in his mind about what he hoped the next several months would bring. There were already murmurs of going back into Iraq if Saddam failed to comply with inspections. The U. N., France, Germany, Russia, China, and others were totally opposed to such a move. *What was the matter with those idiots?* He realized for the umpteenth time he needed to speed up his own plans and execution of his fourth decision. He had begun coding his plans as "Project KAMTAP", an acronym for 'Kill As Many Terrorist As Possible'. No, this wasn't Christian at all.

His praying lately was different than it had been before 9-11. Back then much of his prayer focus was on many of the things a serious Christian would deal with: 'Father help me be a better person. Help me be closer to and more like Jesus. Father help me be a good witness, and help me direct my life to bringing others to You.' Now his prayers also included, 'Father, help me do your will. Help me carry out the plans you've put before me. Help me succeed in this mission you've given me.'

In Toby's mind KAMTAP was indeed a directive of God. But, was it? He had already spent many an hour in prayer and meditation trying to completely validate God's control of KAMTAP. His objective in these sessions was to assure himself that KAMTAP wasn't the psychotic upheaval of a way over-wound, old man, that his planning of KAMTAP truly was the spirit and will of God working through him. So far he'd seen nothing in God's responses or signs that were contrary to the direction his KAMTAP plans were going, and now, thanks to Coon Dog, he finally was able to see the exact path KAMTAP would take. Clearly God had put Coon Dog in Toby's life just for that purpose.

The night became blacker still. He was in the hill country on I-75 between the Appalachian Mountains and the Tennessee River Valley. His truck, along with the other trucks on the highway, had become one with the road. They moved over the interstate in a ballet of speed and steel, always cognizant of each others' movements. Each driver was feeling as if there was nothing more important than to keep eighteen wheels rolling, keep the dance moving, keep rolling, always rolling.

Toby scanned his gauges and switches, stretched, readjusted his seat and the steering wheel in relation to it. Then he reached up, turned the squelch back on the CB radio, and turned the volume up. He thought he'd listen to the mindless prattle that usually dominated the airwaves.

"How 'bout cha', northbound? You copy?"

"Yeah, come on," Toby responded.

"Whatcha leave behind ya?"

"Lemme' see. There's a four wheeler on the shoulder, your side at the forty-two, and a full grown in the middle at the thirty-six."

"'Preciate that. You lookin' good back to K'town ceptin' for some crazy preacher down on channel seven. He probably be a' runnin' yore front door bout' ten mile up."

"Appreciate it driver. You have a good one."

"Ten-four, you do the same."

Toby continued listening in on a dozen different trucker conversations over the next half hour but didn't key his mike. He was content to simply listen. It helped divert, if only for a few minutes, his preoccupation with KAMTAP. Then between the crackle and static and between the many stronger signals from other transmitters on channel nineteen, all vying for his ear, he picked out a distinctive voice which although it was carried by a very weak signal, seemed to be aimed at him personally.

"Make no mistake about it sinners, it ain't too late to get right with...", and the static broke up whatever followed. Then a moment later, "Whatever ails you, whatever torment and temptation Satan throws at you, it can be overcome. Jesus Christ will..." and the signal faltered.

Toby could make out only bits and pieces of the communication, but then the signal strength increased and within two minutes he was able to hear clearly, "You're listening to the Christian Truck Driver Ministry. If you are in need of prayer, if you feel lost and don't know where to turn, or if you are unsaved and want to do something about it, then please drop down to channel 7," and the voice left channel 19. Toby realized this must be the crazy preacher the driver warned him about. This preacher didn't sound all that crazy to Toby, and he reached up to the CB and moved the channel selector to 7.

"Thank you drivers, those of you that just tuned in channel 7. It's better we get off 19 when we're talking and praying. It's better to be on God's channel – channel 7. You are listening to the Christian Truck Driver's Ministry. The purpose of this ministry is to pray for and pray with truck drivers. Also, if you are a driver who hasn't been saved by the blood of Jesus, and you can't go on the way you are, then tonight your life may change. It will change if you want Jesus to take you. Now drivers, I'm going to pray for us all, and please jump in and pray with me when the spirit moves you. Heavenly Father, we come unto Your presence tonight, humble truck drivers all, humble servants all. We pray You will guide us safely through this dark night and get us to our destination without hurting anyone. We pray You will be with each driver out here tonight and that Your hands be on the wheel with ours. We pray You will be with each driver's family, and protect them and keep them strong while we are gone. Father we pray for the souls of each and every driver out here tonight; that they know Jesus as their Lord and Savior. Father, we pray that if there is a special need, a special situation that any driver is agonizing over tonight, well Father, we pray that Your spirit be with that driver tonight and bring him comfort and that Your Spirit will provide a special blessing to that driver, no matter how difficult or impossible it may seem. Father, we ask these things in the name of Jesus Christ, our Lord and Savior. Amen."

Two separate mikes broke in on channel 7, each with a reverent "Amen", and Toby realized he hadn't been the only person listening to the prayer. What struck Toby was the feeling of absolute sincerity intoned by the preacher's voice and delivery. The resonance, the power in that voice nearly overwhelmed Toby. He had to catch his breath and ponder what he just heard. If there was a voice on this Earth that could have been the voice of Moses, surely this voice was it. Even more, it might have been the voice of an educated, Appalachian Moses. It possessed the raw emotion and twang of the old time mountain evangelicals, at the same time smooth, sophisticated, and authoritative. Toby never heard anything like it before. He had to respond in some way. He keyed his mike, "Preacher, you got a copy?"

"I'm not a preacher, just a truck driver wanting to do God's will. And how about you, driver? I've got a feeling you're wanting to do God's will also."

Toby reflexively tapped his brakes and thought about stopping. He might be better off to just let this new CB signal get on down the road and fade away. There was something a little too eerie about this guy seemingly reading Toby's mind.

"Thinking about stopping? I saw you tap your brakes."

I don't believe it! How did he know that? Then Toby realized the strange CB voice must have been in one of the two or three trucks he had just passed. "No, I'm not stopping. You just surprised me. That's all."

The voice like Moses came back even stronger this time, "So, how about it, Toby, are you wanting to do God's will?"

That was it! That was enough! "Listen you son of a bitch! I don't know who you are, but I suggest you take your bullshit and your circus tent preaching on down the road, and leave me alone."

"Toby, I'm not trying to alarm you or freak you out. I don't really know how I knew your name. Sometimes these things just happen to me. I can't explain it."

Toby again was captured by the caring and sincerity in the voice and couldn't for the life of him throw another verbal attack back at the other driver.

For a minute there was only static and crackle on the CB then the voice came back, "Look, this is hard to explain. I told you I'm not a preacher. I'm not, but I have certain visions, certain premonitions. Tonight I felt your presence approaching me. Every night, wherever I am, I pray for drivers. Sometimes I sense a certain need or a certain direction God takes me in prayer. I don't know why, but as you approached, as you got closer to me, I sensed you were listening, and I sensed very strongly that you are involved in something which you feel is directing you to do God's will. As for how I know your name, I can't explain it."

Toby didn't say anything, and again, other than the crackle of static on the empty air wave, there was silence for a minute or so.

Now, the voice, more subdued and having also taken on a more considerate tone, came back, "I think the thing to do now is to put this encounter we've had back in God's hands. You're about out of range now I'm sure, but if you still hear me,

I'm just going to say I'll be praying for you Toby. If it is God's will for us to run into each other again, that's exactly what will happen. May your heart find peace in your struggle."

As Toby sped away, his mind was an awful clutter. This was not what he needed. An encounter with a mystic psycho who could practically read his mind; and the fact that God somehow gave him Toby's name was more than spooky. He raced on through Tennessee and into Virginia on I-81.

South of Staunton, Va., Toby began to search for a place to stop and sleep. The famous Whites Truck Stop was filled up, so he went on northward and tried two more truck stops, again with no luck. He was getting more frustrated by the minute, but there was nothing he could do except continue driving north until something opened up. He asked himself, 'Why not just park along the shoulder on an exit or entrance ramp?' No, the Virginia State Troopers, unlike those in some other states, would ticket truckers attempting to sleep on an interstate ramp. He wondered if experienced drivers had the same trouble he did almost every night – trying to find a parking spot to sleep in? He suspected they didn't, and he was correct. The experienced drivers had been 'out there' so long that they knew every conceivable parking spot for thousands of miles. They knew the little country diners three miles off the interstate where around back behind the dumpster and next to the trailer park there was room enough to squeeze in five trucks, if you didn't mind negotiating the knee deep potholes with big chunks of broken ice floating in them in winter or mosquitoes swarming around them in the summer. They knew the access roads to the factories and plants where you'd usually find six or seven trucks parked outside in dusty pull-over areas or trashy shoulders. In many of these you could expect that a prostitute would wake you by tapping or sometimes beating on your locked door. The experienced drivers knew which of the few malls and other retail centers allowed big trucks to park, and the ones that didn't. But Toby was learning. In a couple of years, if he was still alive and still driving, he would know enough of those places to make his life much easier.

Tonight, however, he was having no luck at all. It was way after midnight now. He was out of legal driving hours, and already he was contemplating a very risky maneuver for a rookie driver – to get off the interstate, head for the nearest small town to search for an empty lot or a pullover – some place that he could park and sleep. First, he checked with another driver on the CB. "Are there any truck stops going north in the next fifty miles?"

"Roger that driver. Two in Harrisonburg up in front of you thirty miles but all the holes are filled up."

"'Preciate it, southbound. You're looking good down to the sixty-four split."

"Ten-four, have a safe trip."

"Back at you driver." He made up his mind, and aimed the truck onto U. S. 250 going into Staunton, Virginia. Driving into town from the east he spotted a couple of possible parking places only to discover that each had *NO TRUCK PARKING – VIOLATORS TOWED* signs posted. He was tired, sleepy, frustrated and fed up. He certainly did not want to go through the courthouse square area that was in the center of every little southern town. There would be civil war statues and war memorials of all kinds, but on this night Toby was in no mood for history.

He spotted a large church parking lot that appeared to be accessible, but by the time he made his mind up to pull in, he'd already driven past it. You get tired, you make mistakes. He was very aware of that little bit of wisdom and was trying to focus so as not to repeat the mistake. Instead, he made a more costly mistake. He decided to turn into a side street he was sure would rap around and back out onto Highway 250, then he'd pull into the church lot from the other direction. The side street turned out to be a trap. It only went into a residential area. He made several turns trying to get back to Highway 250 but only succeeded in finding himself on a narrow one way back road. He was now very, very upset. He had no choice but to back it out and try again. After nearly a half hour, he found his way back to highway 250 and finally turned into the church parking lot. The night was black and cold; a mixed bag of rain, sleet, and snow was just starting to get organized. He got out of the cab to relieve himself, got back in, ate a peanut butter and jelly sandwich, drank cold milk from the jug, and set the optimum idle on the truck so that the cab temperature would remain at sixty-two all night.

Exhausted, he fell into the bunk in the sleeper, but it would take him a half hour to relax enough to fall off to a fretful sleep. His tormented dreams featured a wild eyed horseman brandishing a silver sword. The horseman was mounted on an even wilder, gargantuan, white stallion and they raced up and down countless rows of parked semi-trailers, each with blood oozing and dripping from its trailer door. The sun would be up in about three hours, or would it? At this point Toby could not have told you. He was a rookie truck driver.

Toby was back in the saddle and rolling north before 9 a. m. He was actually up by 7:30 but spent an hour trying to free up his brakes which had frozen thanks to the rain, sleet, snow, and falling temperatures. This section of Virginia was famous for hasty, angry, winter storms. Not only could their ferocity and swiftness surprise you, but many times they chose mid or late fall as well as mid or late spring to strike. Not far from where Toby was, in the tiny hamlet of Grottoes, Va., there was recorded on the 12th of October in 1983 a completely unpredicted snowfall of seventeen inches in less than eight hours. The Allegheny and Shenandoah Mountains to the west and the Blue Ridge Mountains to the east sometimes provided a natural funnel to usher southward these violent storms coming out of Pennsylvania and West Virginia. The ordinary three to five inch snowstorms usually tracked this same Shenandoah Valley corridor but came from the southwest, out of Tennessee.

Toby spotted a handful of four-wheelers which had slid off into the ditches on his short two mile run back to the interstate. He was hoping that the state salt shakers had been out on I-81 early enough to melt the ice out there. The chatter on the CB confirmed that they had, but that further north it was real bad. 'Oh well', Toby thought, 'I'm an old hand at driving in ice and snow'. In reality, he'd been through three snowstorms and had had little or no trouble, except that night in Colorado, but on ice, with eighty thousand pounds, he was still a virgin. As he wove into traffic on I-81 he knew instinctively it was going to be a long day. Traffic was limited to one lane and was doing no more than fifty mph. The hammer lane was packed snow, and only a few big trucks ventured out on it to pass. Most trucks and four wheelers were content to struggle along in the granny lane where there was still a semblance of two narrow pavement corridors.

Two hours later and only seventy miles further north, conditions had become nearly undrivable. There was little traffic moving, and now the entire interstate in both directions was the victim of three inches of packed snow and ice. The farmland adjacent to I-81 was shivering under nearly eight inches. Toby had been on full driving alert. There was nothing on inside the cab to distract him. He even kept the CB off except for a minute or so every ten minutes to listen for weather or road condition information. His nerves were tingling. You could have sliced his anxiety and stress with a knife. Then he saw something that might have been out of a dream. He was approaching the I-66 split to Washington D. C., and for a short stretch the road had widened to five lanes. He had only been going maybe twenty miles per hour when he noticed a couple of four wheelers starting to scoot past him on the left side. There was no telling what lanes any of them were actually in. The roadway was a sheet of glistening whiteness. About the time the first vehicle, a big green SUV, cleared Toby by a mere thirty feet, the lady driving it became the unwanted recipient of multiple, totally out of control three hundred-sixty degree spin-outs which carried her across Toby's path and presumably all the way across the hidden five lanes under the glistening whiteness. It all happened in a matter of two or three seconds, but to Toby it seemed like slow motion. The depiction of 'stop frame vision' was more than appropriate in this case. Toby's comprehension of the event was as if he were watching a dancer gracefully sliding across the floor without a care in the world. The SUV seemed so light and so unaware of what waited for it on the other side as it continued to spin, not slowly and not rapidly, just spin and spin all the way across Toby' field of awestruck vision. The only incongruous element in this dreamlike vision was the panic the lady driving the SUV exhibited. Her fruitless efforts to command the vehicle back into control by pulling frantically at the steering wheel in both directions would have, in a different setting perhaps, been comical. Toby never knew the outcome of the spin out or the fate of the lady. His pre-occupation with his eighty-thousand pounds of trouble overshadowed everything, even this bizarre dreamlike front row vantage of the hapless SUV lady in the never ending spin-out. Then, thirty seconds later it happened again, exactly the same way, only this time the big SUV was red. Toby might have lost his nerve in witnessing both spin-outs and hit his own brakes, but he didn't. He would phone Sarah tonight and tell her what was certainly a most improbable story of the two SUV spin-outs that nearly took him with them. For now, he decided it was time to get off the interstate. Conditions weren't about to improve anytime soon.

He found an exit ramp a couple of miles north of the I-66 split and was able to squeeze his truck in between two NO PARKING signs on the snow-buried shoulder. Surely, under these conditions, the State Troopers wouldn't chase him out. He was right. They were way too busy with accidents and vehicles in ditches.

As the day passed, Toby caught a couple hours of sleep. Then, near sundown, he zipped up his winter coat and ventured out of the cab to walk a mile or two. He found a little greasy spoon diner. He had coffee and two bowls of chili, and then he slogged back through the snow, ice, and slush. He climbed back in the truck. Since the interstate was moving at a better clip now, he prepared to get rolling again.

Toby didn't like night driving, especially in snow and ice, but he was determined to make up the hours he had lost, so he settled into the monotony of going slow and leaving plenty of cushion between him and whatever was in front of him. He knew that the further north he went the better the roads would be. The northern states did a much better job keeping the interstates drivable in winter storms than did the southern states. He drove through the forty-three mile stretch of Maryland averaging forty mph, but was able to speed up to fifty-five mph by the time he was near Harrisburg, Pa. It was getting near 9 p.m. and mother nature told him it was time to find a restroom. Toby spotted a truck stop, topped off his fuel tanks, then pulled the truck up past the fuel pumps which allowed the truck behind him to be fueling while Toby went inside to pay for the fuel and attend to Mother Nature. A few minutes later he was at the cash register paying for a half gallon of milk and some candy bars.

"Hey Toby, is that you?"

Toby turned and was surprised to see Danny Barber standing behind him. "Hey Danny, how's it going?" Danny Barber's father owned a small trucking company back in Lake Thomas, and Danny helped out from time to time. Danny was also Chelsea Barber's father.

"Dad had a couple of drivers quit on him, and we had a hot load that had to be in Philly this morning. How you been doing man? I heard you left the golf course and started driving a big truck. How are you liking it so far?" Toby gave a non-committal shrug of his shoulders and started to say he liked it fine, but Danny continued. "I hated to hear about the trouble you had with Billy Waynick, but the way I understand it, he deserved what he got."

"What are you talking about?"

"You know. That day Chelsea was supposed to have played a practice round with Carolyn and you nearly beat Billy to death. I would have done the same thing. Heck, it could have been Chelsea. Believe me Toby, they ain't nobody in Lake Thomas, that is, those that knew about it, that ever said a bad word about you for what you did."

Toby never knew Danny very well but never did particularly like him. There was something about his manner that just flat irritated people. "What exactly did I do?"

"Come on Toby, you don't have to play it like this with me. I figured when Chelsea told me that Coon Dog just happened, strictly by coincidence, to be in the woods that day and rushed Billy off to the hospital, well I figured I knew what really happened."

"Hold on a minute." Toby paid for his milk and candy and walked Danny over to a corner near the big window looking out at all the trucks lined up at the fuel island. His strong hand had a firm grip on Danny's arm. "Okay, now," Toby said, "Why don't you tell me what really happened?"

Danny began to realize he was in the presence of a dangerous man. "Toby, I told you, nobody blames you for anything. Maybe I ought to get movin' on down the road." Danny didn't want to look directly into Toby's eyes, but even at a glance, he could see that he wanted no part of what was in them. "Okay, okay man, here's the way I figured it. When you got back to the golf course and checked the player registry, you saw that Chelsea didn't show up and that Carolyn was playing alone. You put your clubs on a cart and went to join Carolyn, only you found Waynick there with her, probably trying to put a move on her. You lost it and beat the crap out of him."

"Go on," Toby said.

"Well, Carolyn probably convinced you to call Coon Dog, so he could get over there and cover your ass. I suppose he crashed the golf cart and made up the story about the brakes going out, because we all know that's what he told Martha Jones."

Toby was thinking it over. There was a missing link. "So, you, all by yourself have done all this figuring, and you figure I beat up Billy Waynick." He paused, then said, "There's something missing from your figuring Danny. How did you come to figure that Billy Waynick was making a move on Carolyn?"

Danny sure didn't want to go down this road, but it was too late now. "Chelsea told me. Well, she didn't exactly tell me that Billy made a move on Carolyn, but then again, she did. I sort of pried it out of her. She told me that when the word got around about Billy's so-called accident, she had asked Carolyn about it. You know, Chelsea knew that Carolyn was there that afternoon. Chelsea said it all sounded fishy to her, and well, you know women, ah, girls, they have a sense about those things. Chelsea told me she just knew that something more than an accident had happened."

"Sounds to me like you're figuring again." Toby burned Danny again with his eyes. "How did she know something more happened?"

Danny took a deep breathe, "Because Carolyn started crying when Chelsea kept up the questions."

Toby didn't say another word to Danny Barber. He turned and walked out the door and went back to his truck. The milk and candy bars were still in the bag on the floor next to Danny Barber where Toby had dropped them.

Chapter Ten

Ronnie Matlock had been drinking when his phone rang. He was hoping tonight would be a good night, a night that he could drop off to sleep with only a quart of whiskey consumed since noon. There were many nights it took more. He let the phone ring and ring. He decided not to answer. It wasn't one of his ex-wives. If it had been, he would have answered. If it had been Toby, he would have answered, but Toby never called him. He always called Toby. All those nights they talked, he had always called Toby.

Toby had heard it all. How Coon Dog's three ex-wives and four ex-live-in girl friends had done him wrong; how each one of them had used him. None of them could see that he, Coon Dog, loved them deeply, but they always accused him of drinking away anything they had ever shared. It was the same story with each of them, staying just long enough for him to get his hopes up, for him to say to himself, 'this is the one, the one that's going to stay and love me back'. And then, they left him with an empty house on a night he expected to come home and see them waiting for him. Yeah, Toby had heard it all. Many nights the one sided conversation had lasted until three in the morning. Many other nights it had not started until three in the morning.

In all of these phone calls the subject changed from Coon Dog's many times shattered love life only one time. Coon Dog had been beyond drunk that night, and the alcohol opened the door to another world – a world of unthinkable fear and terror. In that world, eighteen and nineteen year olds carried M-16's, grenades, and claymore mines. A year before they had worn Bermuda shorts, madras shirts, and loafers with no socks; and they raced their cars on dark quarter-mile straights around the edges of American cities. The country boys drank their beer on Friday and Saturday nights at a swimming hole. The city boys drank anywhere. All of the boys who joined up or were drafted were to undergo changes they wouldn't understand for years, some never would.

That night Coon Dog took Toby back thirty years to Vietnam. His Seal squad was being airlifted into North Vietnam on a secret recon mission. The chopper was flying out over the South China Sea at night and made landfall forty miles north of the DMZ. Fifteen minutes later, as the chopper was preparing for insertion, it was shot down. Coon Dog and one other Seal survived the crash. Coon Dog was unconscious until morning, and the other Seal was fatally injured. He died two days later. When Coon Dog became conscious he was immediately beaten, ridiculed, and then locked in a bamboo cage. He received no food or water until the next day. From that day until the fourteenth day of his captivity a predictable routine was established. Shortly after sun-up a guard would unlock the chain on the cage door, open it, and place inside a small tin cup of water and a small bowl of half cooked rice. Around noon a guard would come back and with the cage still locked make Coon Dog first take off his pants, then put his hands behind him up close to the bars. The guard reached in and bound his wrist together with twine, then unlocked the chain and opened the door, put a rope around Coon Dog's neck and cinched it down tightly. He violently dragged him out of the cage by his neck until he could get to his feet, then led him off fifty feet or so into the jungle to give him an opportunity to relieve himself. There was no concern about hygiene. Coon Dog, without the use of his hands, simply had to squat as best he could and try to relieve himself. He would be dragged back to the cage usually to the taunts and beatings of other guards. Sometimes he was blindfolded before being put back in the cage. Sometimes he wasn't. It depended on whether or not they were doing anything in camp that day that they may not have wanted him to see; equipment moving through, troop strength, etc. No attention was given to him until the next morning and the same routine started again.

These were days that would haunt Petty Officer Second Class Ronnie Matlock for the rest of his life. He spent his days and nights daydreaming about food. In his mind he would go through great mounds of every kind of food he'd ever tasted. Then he'd go through all of the fine foods he'd always heard about but had not experienced. He slept very little, but when he was fortunate enough to do so his dreams always included images of his daddy, Horace Matlock. Coon Dog could see himself with Horace out on a thicket covered hillside in early December. A fence line two hundred yards off to their left and a winter tree line about the same distance off to the right. They were rabbit hunting this morning without the dogs. Horace had loaned them out to some friends for the weekend. Coon Dog liked these hunts the best – just him and daddy. He would play the role of the beagle hound rabbit dogs; he would go through the thickest part of the thistles, blackberry briars, cedar groves, knee high light brown meadow grass and downed timber piles which he would rattle with all his weight to scare out a hiding rabbit. He learned at an early age to gut, skin, and clean; rabbit, squirrel, dove, quail, turkey, and deer.

In his bamboo jungle prison cell dreams he saw himself and his daddy doing these things together, and when he awoke he knew he would survive because of these things his daddy had taught him.

On the ninth day of his captivity the guard came to his cage at sun-up, unlocked the chain, opened the door, and placed the water and rice inside. He was closing the door when a single chop stick of the pair he had in a pocket caught on a piece of the bamboo cage and slipped out of his pocket onto the ground. The guard never noticed, locked the chain, and walked away. Coon Dog had noticed when the chopstick fell but waited three hours to make sure the guard wasn't going to return for it, or worse, maybe was baiting him. When he was convinced that neither of these two possibilities were going to take place, he put the fingers of his left hand through the opening at the bottom of the cage. By gently maneuvering the chop stick he was able to lever it high enough to grab it with his other hand and bring it in the cage. He found a notch on a lower bamboo bar and was able to hide it there. After sundown he picked it up and examined it carefully with his hands. The wood wasn't oak or hickory, but if he was careful he thought it might be hard enough, rigid enough to be worked into the lethal weapon he would use to thrust through the neck and throat of an unsuspecting guard.

The next day as he was being dragged and walked out to his jungle outhouse, Coon Dog paid particular attention to the jungle floor around his squatting area. As the guard turned away Coon Dog feigned a stumble. He hit the ground hard and before the guard could turn to see what happened, Coon Dog had seemingly bit at the ground with his mouth. The guard turned on him and spit out a stream of Vietnamese obscenities, then beat him severely with the butt of his rifle. The guard continued the verbal and physical assault on Coon Dog as he dragged and prodded him back to his bamboo cage. Finally, a half hour later, after his hands had been freed and with none of the guards close by or watching him, Coon Dog removed the prize from his mouth. It was a thin rock with one very thin edge. The rock was two inches long and maybe an inch and a half wide. He hid it as best he could and waited until dark to begin using it to sharpen the chop stick. That night and the following four nights he scratched, ground, and scraped at the narrow end of the chopstick. He worked very slowly and had to be careful not to make any noise. On the last night he had the point sharp enough to prick his own finger and produce a drop of blood.

Sunrise on the fourteenth day of Coon Dog's captivity in North Vietnam was two hours away. Coon Dog was mentally rehearsing the killing he planned on doing at sun-up. If he could do it with no noise and if good fortune would intervene by having no other guards nearby, he just might make it out alive. He was more than willing to risk death. It would be far better than the alternative fate that would unfold any day now—being transferred to Hanoi. As the time drew near, Coon Dog's focus and resolve intensified. The eastern horizon first allowed a narrow gray band to emerge then to blend with the lightest pink imaginable, broken here and there by heavy clouds. Monkeys began squawking somewhere deep in the jungle, and a dog barked closer. The camp was stirring. Coon Dog had his weapon under his right forearm, holding it there with pressure from his fingers. The approaching guard had the tin cup of water and bowl of rice with him. He bent down and placed them on the ground, unlocked the chain and opened the door. Coon Dog waited. There weren't any other guards around. The guard picked up the cup and bowl and leaned forward to place them down inside the cage.

Coon Dog's timing was perfect. His left hand went to the guard's mouth, he jammed his fingers into the guard's mouth literally half way down his throat. His thumb was a relentless steel piston clawing at the soft pallet area under the floor of the mouth, clawing at it from the outside, clawing at the flesh in the middle of the semicircular mandible. With the guard's head and neck totally under control, Coon Dog jerked the head up violently, stretching the neck to the maximum. At this point the anatomy studies Coon Dog had been performing on his own neck, particularly the larynx, were about to pay dividends. He quickly brought the shank to the V point just above the middle of the collarbone and just below the larynx. Careful not to break it, he forced it through the skin and then deeper until it perforated the wind pipe. His intent was to tear a hole big enough to get his thumb in and do real damage. Coon Dog's left hand vice grip in the guard's mouth and under his pallet ratcheted up a couple of notches taking the guards head to the top of the cage. Two more controlled jabs with the shank gave Coon Dog enough of a hole in the guard's neck for Coon Dog to push his right thumb in and wreak havoc on not only the windpipe, but the larynx also. There would be no screaming from this guard. Then and only then did Coon Dog remove his left hand from the guards mouth. He put it on the guards head, grabbed all the hair he could find and brought the guards neck down violently across his knee, quickly turned the guard and brought the head down again. Perforated wind pipe, destroyed larynx, and broken neck. Coon Dog wasted no more time in his cage, went through the guard's pockets, found nothing, and slipped into the jungle.

In less than three weeks Petty Officer second class, Ronnie Matlock, USN had worked his way far enough south to hear U.S. Marine artillery fire bases sounding off near the DMZ. He had survived on insects and three snakes that he had killed. He was able to open the snakes up with a shard of steel he found near a downed U.S. aircraft. He fashioned a new shank with his find; this one actually closer to a machete. The blade was around fourteen inches long with a solid mangrove handle secured with an eighth of an inch thick vine cord. In the United States this weapon-tool could have sold for forty dollars. With the belly side of the snakes opened from head to tail, he cleaned his meals in streams and ate everything to the bone with the exception of the toughest of the back skin. Having got close to the U.S. troops, his job now was to not get shot by a friendly. His plan was to stay hidden until he spotted squad or platoon strength marines on patrol. He'd let them get settled into a night position, observe their placement of claymores, and crawl undetected right into the marine camp. It all worked to perfection, and at daybreak two members of Delta squad were amazed when they awoke and found the wildest looking U.S. fighting man they had ever seen. Coon Dog was curled up between them, sleeping like a baby.

Again Coon Dog's phone rang and he thought to himself it may have been the same caller from twenty minutes ago that he chose not to answer. *What the hell?* "Hello."

"Coon Dog, this is Toby."

"You are kidding me. I could of swore it was Nakita Chruszhev. I know you are".

"Save it for another time. I'm going to ask you this one time. What happened on the golf course that day you took Billy Waynick to the hospital?"

Coon Dog said, "Wait just a minute. I'll be right back." He went to the kitchen sink, ran the cold water, and splashed it all over his head, face, and neck trying to jump start his whiskey clouded mind. He dried with a towel and went back to the phone. "Toby, whata' you talkin' about?"

"I told you, I'm only going to ask you this but one time, and I've already done that. Now, talk to me, and tell me what happened."

Coon Dog knew that if he told him, he would probably be signing Billy's death certificate for sure and maybe Toby's. He'd try stalling; he knew it would be a mistake to tell him. "I thought you knew the details back then. There ain't much I can add. I heard the crash, come out of the woods, seen Billy on the ground, and took him to the hospital. That's about all there was to it."

"No, that's not all there was to it. I want it all, Coon Dog!" Toby's voice was resolute and sounded as if he was prepared to continue as long as it took to get what he wanted.

Coon Dog didn't respond, and finally Toby said, "We are going to get this done, Coon Dog. I promise you, we are going to get it done. You can save us both a lot of trouble. Just go ahead and tell me, and tell me. NOW!"

"Toby, I don't know what to say. I've told you everything already."

It was becoming clear Toby would have to lead. "You say you came out of the woods and saw Billy on the ground. Where was Carolyn?"

"I guess she was somewhere way on down past number four. I'm sure she would have come to help if she'd known somebody got hurt."

Toby's memory traveled back some four months or so, and he went over all he remembered that day. "So, while you were taking Billy to the hospital, Carolyn was somewhere past number four on her way to completing the first nine. Right? She wasn't anywhere near Waynick when he crashed. Is that it?"

Coon Dog thought an opportunity to keep the lid on might be presenting itself. "Sure," he said. "You and me both know she would have come back to help if she knew anybody was hurt."

"Right, you already said that." But Toby wasn't finished. "So, she was past number four and evidently a good ways past it because she didn't hear the crash, and we know she didn't hear because she would have come back if she had. Is that it?"

There was a tone in Toby's voice that told Coon Dog he was about to be had, and he was sensing that the opportunity to keep the lid on was slipping away. "Yeah, I reckon that's it. What more could there be?"

Toby responded, "Okay, so she didn't hear or see anything and continues on playing out her round. She finished, gets in her car and drives home. Right? You with me? That's all there was to it. She never saw Waynick and nothing happened between them. Right?" Toby waited for Coon Dog.

"Sure," Coon Dog said.

"Then if she completes her round, let's say she didn't even play eighteen, only nine, then if she started at 3:30, if she only played nine, she would have finished no earlier than five. That all sounds straight. Right, Coon Dog?" Again he waited for Coon Dog's response. Coon Dog didn't say anything.

Toby went on, "The only problem with that is the fact that I know Carolyn was home by 4:45 or so because I went straight home that afternoon from a buying trip down in Wayne County. When I got home Carolyn was there. I didn't see her; she was in her room, but I know she was there because her car was there. So, therefore, she didn't complete even nine holes. I also know that some time after that day, when Chelsea pushed her, she was crying about what actually happened." He paused a moment and went on, "Whatever Waynick did to Carolyn that day had to be bad for you to have busted him up the way you did. I talked to the doctor the next day, the doctor that patched him up. He probably should have stayed in the hospital for a week instead of hightailing it off to the Caribbean like he did. I see now why he did it, but I tell you this, Coon Dog, the son of a bitch ain't going to hide no more," and Toby snapped his cell phone shut, put the truck in gear, and headed off into the awful night..

Chapter Eleven

Toby's next load assignment was coming in on the qualcom. A blinking light indicated the reception of a new message. He placed the small computer on his lap and read the instructions Mountaintop Transport had just sent him. From Syracuse they had him taking a load to Burlington, Vermont where they had him picking up another load going down to Brooklyn, New York. When they got a rookie driver up in the northeast, they would keep him there until the driver demanded a trip back home. For most trucking companies there would be no consideration of a trip back home for at least fourteen days, sometimes longer. Mountaintop Transport was no different. Toby's desire to get back home and have a little one on one session with Billy Waynick was growing into a burning rage, but as always with Toby, it was concealed very well.

After his phone call to Coon Dog last night, he had nearly turned the truck south and started back for home, but he didn't. He had driven all the way through Pennsylvania and well into New York before he parked the truck at 3:30 in the morning. His dreams, however, were out of control. He saw thousands of shaved head prisoners being herded up a steep mountain to a certain death. At the top each one was ritually placed on a grassy area at the edge of a drop-off into blackness. Then a monster, fifty feet tall swung a grotesque golf club and drove them over the edge into the blackness.

Suddenly, Toby realized he was one of the victims and was in free fall in the blackness and eventually noticed others floating past him. Some were playing stringed instruments, some were reading the bible, and some were trying to claw their way back to the top of the mountain. If he hit bottom Toby knew he would be dead. Just then he awoke in a cold sweat. The whole night went the same way. Awake or asleep, there was no peace for Toby.

He started driving at seven that morning and was in Syracuse with his load delivered by 11:00 a.m. He filled his coffee thermos at a truck stop and was eastbound towards Burlington. There was plenty of snow in up state New York, but as he knew it would, most of it was stacked into three and four foot high piles on both sides of the pavement. He would see it six and seven feet high away from the interstate where it had drifted against fencing and structures; but he was warm and cozy in his cab, drinking the coffee like it was life itself.

He made the shipper in Burlington before midnight. He dropped his empty trailer on an icy pad then went to door number '35' on the east side of the warehouse and lined up the tractor to back in under his load. He was tired and tormented, not only by his incomplete planning on the fourth decision, but now by his vengeful intentions to deal with Billy Waynick. He should have been more focused on what he was doing, but he was having a hard time. As he slowly backed under the waiting trailer, he didn't feel or hear the solid 'click' that told him the locking arm on the fifth wheel had caught the kingpin securely. Instead, he felt a bump and heard a grind. The landing gear on the trailer were extended nearly all the way, as a result it lifted the trailer higher than normal, thus he went right under the kingpin and his tires came to rest against the landing gear. He got out to see if there was any damage and also to see if he could pull up and clear the kingpin. If so, he could crank the landing gear up a few inches and start again. But as he pulled up to clear the kingpin, he felt the fifth wheel catch on it from the wrong side and knew he would have to crank the landing gear down as far as possible in order to pull up successfully. After ten minutes of arduous labor he exhausted himself and knew he had the landing gear extended as far as possible. It wasn't far enough. He would need a helper to hold the forward part of the fifth wheel down with a two by four or something similar while he again attempted the pull-up. Fortunately, one of the other drivers saw his predicament and came to help. After another half hour, they succeeded in getting him out of the jam.

The entire episode only cost him forty-five minutes, but it was just one more problem that had popped up on this trip. First, there had been the crazy preacher. Then, there was the lost time in Staunton, VA. Then, the snowstorm. Next, Toby had received the bombshell about Billy Waynick. And now, this. It was 1:00 a.m. Toby had slept sixteen hours in the last three days, really not bad at all, but now he was heading for the worst place in the world if you were a rookie truck driver, New York City. It was the equivalent of a mountain climber facing Everest on one leg, or a swimmer crossing the English Channel with no wet suit, or a scraggly, mangy stray dog expecting any kindness as it starves and wanders around the empty, dirty streets of downtown Detroit. Sleep deprivation's deadliest results sometimes don't happen instantly. The damage can be cumulative, and by the time Toby's duties had been completed in New York, he would be reduced nearly to watermelon pulp.

Truck drivers have been telling stories about their adventures in New York City for as long as trucks have been going there. The first and most obvious problem is the congestion. It's nothing to sit in traffic for an hour and maybe travel two city blocks. On a good day you must allow at least two hours to get from interstate 95 to any of the five boroughs with the exception of Staten Island which should normally be made in under an hour. If your destination is somewhere out on Long Island, you automatically increase the two hour minimum to three hours or longer. The second most obvious problem are the streets themselves. They were never designed to accommodate seventy-two foot tractor trailers. The streets are narrow. They are loaded with potholes. There is no parking. Accurate signs and directions are more often than not, non- existent or missing in action. Add to all this, there are countless restrictions on where trucks can go. They can't enter a designated 'parkway'. Trucks can't go under many of the train and freeway overpasses. And they are restricted from many areas for security reasons.

Not as obvious but equally problematic to rookie truck drivers, is the fact that many of the warehouses and shipping docks are operated by union labor. This means you may wait anywhere from two hours to ten hours or more to be loaded or unloaded. Another obvious obstacle to rookies is the cultural chasm. Simply communicating is often difficult. A rookie truck driver from the Deep South can easily be overwhelmed trying to understand Puerto Ricans, Mexicans, Chinese, Slavs, and so on. New York City for a rookie truck driver is the kind of place you absolutely dread going to. It's the kind of place that even if you do everything perfectly, you are still likely to get into trouble.

Toby drove three hours and finally began looking for a parking place. He was in Massachusetts, and he spotted a construction area maybe a quarter mile off the interstate. He missed the exit and had to drive twelve miles to the next one, turn around and come back. There were several other trucks in the construction area. They too, were using it as a parking lot in order to catch a couple of hours of sleep. He lucked out tonight, and it was a good thing he did. He was going to need all the luck he could get. Toby Etheridge was a rookie truck driver preparing to navigate New York City for only the second time by himself. Dave, his Mountaintop Transport trainer, had gone in with him twice and pulled him out of certain trouble both times. Toby's only solo trip into the city left him declaring he would never go into 'that stinking hell hole' again, but he knew he would be required to if he intended to stay with the company, and he had to stay with the company in order to carry out his plans for the fourth decision.

Toby's internal alarm clock had him stirring around in the sleeper berth shortly after sunrise. His sleep had again been a fitful, energy sucking episode of futility. A parade of maddening images of 9-11 rumbled through his tormented dreams. He witnessed the twin towers come down an atom at a time. It was a never ending destruction of America's power seemingly at the molecular level. The debris finally coming to a steamy, fiery rest in a horrid cesspool of blood and yellowish, greenish slime which bubbled up from its wretched entrails the burnt and broken faces of the victims.

When Toby was fully awake he was so mad and so spent he struck out at the walls of the sleeper berth, and actually kicked so hard he tore the door off the lower storage compartment between the sleeper and the front seats. He knew he had to get out of the truck before he tore it up. As soon as he was dressed he grabbed a water bottle, left the truck, and headed off on foot for a wooded hilly area he spotted a half mile away. Deep in the woods after a twenty minute hike, he fell to his knees, took a long drink from the water bottle and poured the rest of the cold water over the back of his head as he knelt over and dropped his head close to the ground. "Father, please help me. I'm in trouble again. I just don't know if I'm going the way You want me to. Please lead me, please guide me. I'm having a tough time with some things right now. Father, I need You to give me strength, to take me and have me do Your will. I can't do it myself; I know that." He paused, took several deep breathes, and continued. "Father, I'm going to need Your help on this thing with Billy Waynick. You know I told him years ago that if he ever tried anything with my family, I'd kill him. Well Father, there's no doubt he's tried something with Carolyn. I don't know what he did and I, well Father, I'm just not sure I won't kill him. You see now, I'm going to need Your help on this. Father, the only thing I ever want is to do Your will. Help me, show me the way." He stopped again, got up and walked for a minute, then looked up into the slowly awakening early morning sky. "Father, I had bad dreams last night, and I sort of lost it this morning when I woke up. Continue to guide me on this terrorist thing I'm working on. Show me what to do and how to do it."

Toby's prayer continued for some time. He made special requests for protection of his family and friends, and a very special petition that God surround Carolyn with all of His love and support and healing. Toby didn't even want to think of exactly what kind of healing was necessary, but whatever kind it was, that his God would provide it for his daughter.

Six hours later Toby was on the Bronx, Whitestone Bridge coming into Queens and wishing there was another way, other than using a big truck, to complete his fourth decision. He turned west on the Long Island Expressway, then southwest on the Brooklyn Queens Expressway. A half hour later he was attempting to fine-tune his focus by taking the correct exit and following the directions he had to the consignee of the load. Focusing was difficult. He was nearly exhausted. But nonetheless, he swung his rig off the expressway into the heart of Brooklyn, New York. He was certain he had the correct exit, but to his consternation the street sign at the end of the ramp did not bear the name his directions said it should have.

Most times, in a situation like this he would have pulled the rig to the shoulder of the ramp and phoned the consignee for clarification, but not here, not today. There was no shoulder. Also, the traffic behind him was already honking for him to move on through the intersection. And that's just what Toby did. He took a left, as his directions ordered, even though the street name didn't match his directions. *My God!*, he thought, *What am I doing here?* The shock a rural Alabaman receives when confronted with the filth and squalor of Brooklyn is similar to a bad dream. You wish you weren't there. Trash was stacked everywhere on the side streets in neighborhoods and on the wider commercial and industrial corridors it was blowing everywhere in the stiff winter wind. Toby wondered where the millions of inhabitants were. There were very few people on the streets he was on.

He drove for several blocks looking for any street name that would match any on his directions but found none. He pulled over as close to the curb as possible, stopped, put his four way blinkers on and actually hoped a cop would stop to harass him. Maybe some accurate directions would be forthcoming. While he waited he double checked the qual-com, and then he phoned the consignee who told him the exit numbers on the expressway had been revised six months ago and that Toby had missed his correct exit. He went on to tell him he could simply turn around, or continue on the street he was on for about three miles until it 'Y' ed and then to stay right for so many blocks, and then to....The connection was barely audible. Toby thanked him and continued on in the wrong direction he was going. He was looking for a place he could swing the big truck around. After a mile, he had no luck but told himself, *I will not turn off this street hoping to do a three-sixty on the side streets, hoping to come out in the right direction on the correct street!* He knew what kind of trouble that could lead to.

After five more blocks he stopped again. After considering the alternatives, he settled on a tactic he was hoping he would not have to choose. He would back the rig into a side street thus enabling him to get the nose turned back in the direction he should have been going. Like a child who stood on the end of the high diving board, and after many minutes of trying to capture enough courage to go ahead and dive off, Toby went two more blocks very slowly. He very carefully eyeballed the next side street to his left, and at the same time scanned his mirrors for cars behind him. Then he dove off. He was attempting the unthinkable. He was going to turn his seventy-two foot long eighteen wheeler around in the heart of Brooklyn by backing into a side street. He could count at least fifty things that could go wrong.

Toby put his four ways on and drove past the side street he had chosen. He pulled the trailer up thirty feet past the street and stopped. There were no cars behind him, but he thought he noticed traffic on the side street coming his way. He got out, jogged back to the intersection and then up the side street about eighty feet with his arms up in a HALT position. The oncoming traffic saw him and heeded the instruction. Toby went to the window of the first car and hurriedly asked the driver to please just sit there a moment to hold traffic behind him so Toby could back his truck into the street. Everything Toby did in the next five minutes was done on instinct and gut reaction. What little planning he had done to pull this maneuver off had already been done. Now he would have to move, react, move, react, on and on, until he got it turned around. He walked back towards his truck, forcing himself to SLOW DOWN, THINK, RELAX. He noticed the traffic behind the truck already getting impatient. Many of the cars were ignoring Toby's plight and drove through the intersection on the green light, swerving out into the opposite traffic lanes on the left to go around the truck.

By the time he got back into the cab, the red light behind him stopped them. It was now or never. He spotted a pick up truck with construction workers in it coming at him from dead ahead. He got back out, stopped them, and got them to hold off traffic in all directions. He got back in the cab and started the backing maneuver to the side street on his left. It was very tight. It appeared he would clear the telephone pole on the corner at the tail of the trailer's blind side by less than a foot. So now with his rig squarely in the middle of the intersection at a forty-five degree angle, he slowly got back out and resolutely walked back to eyeball the actual clearance he had. It was eight inches. That would be enough.

Toby was now caught up in the drama of the situation. He could hear horns honking from all four directions, and it only bolstered his resolve not to get in a hurry and make a mistake-not to hit something. He even relished the fact that his truck was the center of attention. He got back in the cab, pulled up maybe ten feet, then put it back into reverse and eased on back the eighty feet to where that first car was. He then slowly aimed it as far left as he could go in the attempt to swing it around that same telephone pole he missed while backing. He had to 'jack' the tractor two times on the far side of the intersection, then turn his right mirror all the way out to watch the right tail end of his trailer miss the telephone pole by five inches. This rookie truck driver had passed the first test of what would surely be multiple tests on this his second solo attempt to conquer The Big Apple. If he hadn't been exhausted he would have been elated over this first victory. Instead, Toby was trying to relax and muster up some energy and mental fortitude. He knew there were more tests ahead. New York City doesn't let a rookie out of her grip that easily.

Toby was back on the track the consignee had given him on the phone. He made the first two turns with no problem, but as he approached what should have been the third turn, he saw the street name didn't match the one he had been given. He stopped in the middle of the street ignoring the traffic he was blocking and dialed up the consignee on his cell phone. He got a different voice in the receiving department than he did on the last phone call. "Willoughby's Brooklyn Warehouse. Whadda' ya' need?" a heavy NYC accent said.

"Yes sir. I've got a load coming to you today. I called a half hour ago for directions and was told to ...." Toby explained the problem again.

The heavy NYC accent came back, "Yeah. You was talking to Roger. He don't know shit. Here's what you need to do."

Toby wasn't surprised at all. He knew anything could and would happen in this hell hole. He got his new directions and realized immediately he was faced with another side street back-in turn around. And, it started snowing, hard. Two hours later Toby turned his big truck into the 'holding pen' of Willoughby's Brooklyn Warehouse. The parking area was outside the fenced, concertina wired facility. Toby parked, got out of the cab, walked through the guard shack and gate to where they required him to produce his truck number, pick up number, and CDL-A driver's license. It was almost dark, and it was still snowing. So far an accumulation of three inches of wet sticky snow was on everything. He walked to the end of the building where he could just make out the 'ING' of the word RECEIVING on a sign. The first five letters of the word were iced and snowed over. Toby's minimal experience with snow had not provided him with anything like this; a snow so wet and sticky it clung to and covered up anything it touched, including vertical, metal signs. Toby went into the receiving office which was little more than a dirty shack. The window on the door leading out into the warehouse dock area was so filmed over with dirt, you couldn't see anything on the other side. A trash can was overflowing in a corner of the room. There were no chairs, only a filthy looking snack machine. A fat man sat at a rusting metal desk on the far side of the room. Toby walked up close enough to where he knew the guy had to be aware of his presence. The large man kept his head buried in the porn magazine he was looking at and gave no recognition of Toby.

"Excuse me sir," Toby was sure the man would look up, but he didn't.

"Leave your paperwork in the tray. When a door opens up we'll call you on channel 13," the fat man said without ever looking up.

Toby went back to the cab, set the CB on channel 13, then laid down on the bunk in the sleeper. He dared not fall asleep. If he missed the messages coming over the channel, there wasn't any telling how long he would be stuck at Willoughby's Brooklyn Warehouse. After three hours of hearing no messages for himself, Toby went back in the receiving office. The fat man had been replaced by another man at the rusting metal desk.

Toby said, "Excuse me sir, I've been waiting about three hours and...."

The man cut Toby off, "Check with Harry. He ought a' be out by dock 18."

Toby's frustration was peaking and a certain kind of anger was setting in. It was not the anger you get when you know for an absolute fact that someone is trying to do you wrong. This anger was the kind when you come across someone you know for an absolute certainty doesn't give a damn about you or the negative circumstances you might be in; as if you didn't even exist.

Toby tried again, "Sir, I don't believe you understand, I...."

"Look Mack, I done told ya'. Harry's the guy you need to see," and he looked at Toby as if he were the most stupid person in the world.

Toby had to suppress what he really wanted to do, instead he said, "The guy here before said to monitor channel 13 for my dock assignment."

"That was Roger. He don't know shit. Anyway, Harry's the union dock foreman. I think they come off break in twenty minutes."

Toby turned and walked out the door to the docks, stopped at door 18 and waited. A horn went off a little later and several workers started moving around. After three tries Toby found Harry and was told he could come in the gate and back his loaded trailer into dock 16. On his way back to the truck Toby checked out the loading dock area from the outside. He'd only been in trucking for four months and two weeks, but he'd never seen a worse dock area than the one he was looking at. Everything was extremely tight. There was no turn-around area. When you made your set up, that was it, and if you required pull-ups you'd be very limited on space. There was a mud bank, now a snow bank with a fence on it that prevented any kind of a big, lazy pull-up. If you required a pull-up you'd have none of the eighty feet or more you'd have in most places. Here you might have forty feet. After the sixth attempt to get the tail end of his trailer in the narrow hole in front of door 16 was successful, he realized that he had not opened his trailer doors. There was less than a foot on each side between his trailer and the two trailers he was between. The advantage he'd been using for four and a half months on keeping his doors closed while backing was now going to exact its toll from this rookie truck driver. He had no choice but to pull out, open the doors, secure them with the tie-down to the catch on each side of the trailer, and start backing in again. He made six or seven attempts, each time exiting the cab and walking over to the blind side to check the clearance he did or did not have. He was thinking he might not have enough left in him to get this done, and he started praying while he was working. On his next attempt he actually got his left side trailer door nudged up against the docked trailer on that side. *Oh no! Here we go. I'm going to tear that door off, get fired, skedaddle back home with my tail between my legs, and I'll have to start all over on my fourth decision.* Then an angel appeared. Another driver who was waiting on Toby so he could get by, came up to Toby's window and said he'd spot him on that far side. He got up front where Toby could see him and gave him hand signals on the clearance. In another ten minutes Toby had the trailer on dock door 16 with the trailer doors open, and no damage to any equipment. Toby thanked the driver for his help. Toby didn't think he would have made it without him. And, he thanked God for sending him.

It was midnight. In the last four days Toby had slept eighteen hours, an average of four and a half a day. He was used to it by now, but this trip was wearing on him in other ways as well. He got on the CB and asked the other drivers if Willoughbys allowed overnight parking in the holding pen? Of course not. He should have known. The snow had continued most of the night, and it was now coming down harder than ever. *I don't have much of a choice. I've got to get out of here and at least make the Pennsylvania line.* His next load was waiting for him at Allentown, Pa., twenty-five miles inside the state line. The qual-com said he had to be there by 8:00 a.m. In normal weather, Toby would not have seen a problem at all, that is, other than finding someplace to park. New Jersey was nearly as bad as New York as far as traffic and congestion and was also very limited in parking for big trucks. *Oh well. Here I go again,* he thought to himself.

As he pulled out of Willoughby's Brooklyn Warehouse he was shocked at what little visibility he had. In a moving vehicle the effects of falling snow intensified, and in the thick, wet snow Toby was in tonight, he had at best thirty–five feet in front of him in which he could actually see anything. Worse, the wet, sticky snow had covered all of the street signs. You couldn't see a thing. He tried to remember the route he'd come in on, and now he was attempting to retrace that route to find a way back to the freeway. He started praying again. He could not pick up the correct trail out. He got on the CB to see if other big trucks were in the vicinity and maybe help him. There was activity on channel '19', even at this early hour in the morning, but no one responded to Toby. He was simply guessing now, and he felt that at any moment he would be at a spot where he couldn't go forward or make any turns. There was no visibility. He was feeling his way along the empty, snow covered streets of Brooklyn. He couldn't see.

Then he thought he caught the weak flicker of a set of tail lights up ahead. He got a little closer and could just make out the ghostly silhouette of the back end of a big trailer. Its brake lights would come on sporadically in the wet slippery snow, and the truck was going very slowly. Toby stayed behind it. *Just maybe this truck, like me, is trying to get over to New Jersey.* Toby had no choice but to go on that gamble. He stayed behind the phantom truck in front of him; the driver never responded to Toby's calls on the CB. In thirty minutes Toby began to see more taillights ahead of him. Eventually he could see he was entering a toll area, and he could just make out the Verrazano Bridge signs which were not yet totally covered by the snow. He swallowed hard. He knew that in a few minutes he would be two hundred feet above the icy Atlantic Ocean. He didn't want to think about it. He'd been over this bridge in good weather. It was a long way down to the water. This was one snowy, icy bridge at 2:00 a.m. in the black, cold morning. He was going to drive over it very slowly. He didn't have to worry about holding up other drivers, they were all creeping along. He finally made it to Staten Island, then to The New Jersey Turnpike. In a short while he turned right onto Route

287 and then west on I-78. He was out of New York City, out of hell itself. The stress and the sleep deprivation of the last few days had really taken its toll.

It was the middle of the night and Toby was again looking for a place to stop and sleep. He had wanted to at least make the Pennsylvania line, another thirty miles, but he had already ditched that plan. He was way beyond drifting down the river out of control. He was in a raging, frothing, foaming ocean storm, torn and tossed by vengeful howling winds, and his ship was sinking fast. He had to find a safe harbor fast. NOW! He couldn't go on. Even though the snow was easing back now, he couldn't see much of anything. It was physically painful to make the effort to look out the windshield. It was more difficult to make decisions, and again, he actually felt a physical pain when a decision was unavoidable. The pain started in the middle of his spine and quickly rolled up to his neck, shoulders, and head. He felt a total blackout was coming at any moment. Mini-blackouts were short-circuiting his thinking, his reactions to the stress, and his driving.

He tried two truck stops about ten miles from the Pennsylvania line. They were filled up, and he knew that even if he found a tight parking place at one of them, he probably didn't have enough left in him to work the truck into the hole. Almost in panic, almost in tears, he took an exit ramp off to what appeared to be a big shopping center parking lot. At the end of the ramp he could see that it wasn't, and instead of risking going on into the small town and hoping to find something, he got right back on Highway 78 west. Everything he did was a struggle – seeing, driving, breathing, and living. Back on the interstate he was thinking that as a last resort he would simply pull over on the shoulder as far as possible and try to catch an hour of sleep, but he didn't even have the energy left to either make the decision or to execute the pull over. It was easier to keep it going slowly in the right lane and hope he wouldn't kill anyone. In a few minutes, he crossed the Pennsylvania state line. He spotted a state rest area, and with little hope that he would find a parking spot, slowly turned in. He'd nearly driven through the truck parking area and had seen nothing. As he was about to re-enter the interstate, he noticed the very last parking spot was empty. He couldn't believe it, but he pulled in anyway.

Toby thought his troubles were over. It was 3:30 in the morning. He didn't have to be at the shipper in Allentown, Pa. until 8:00. He'd catch three or four hours sleep and make it to the shipper on time. Toby was wrong. He couldn't sleep, and worse, when he lay down on the bunk to try, the walls in the tiny sleeping compartment came crashing in on him. A full blown panic attack was setting in. This time Toby recognized it but was utterly helpless in stemming it's horrendous attack. Yes, he recognized the pressure coming in from all sides, and the complete feeling of helplessness. *You can't do anything to stop it,* he thought. *Somehow, I'll just have to ride it out. But I can't. I'm slipping over the edge. I'm going over. I'm going over now. Goodbye sanity. Maybe I'm already gone. Maybe I've been gone. Yeah, I can see it now. They find a trucker dead in the sleeper. Squashed by unknown forces. No, not unknown. I know what's trying to get me. No doubt, I know what it is. I just wish I could fight it, but I can't. I'm going over now. My God! Why is this cab coming down on me? Why is my chest imploding? Poor Sarah, it will be hard on her. It wouldn't be so bad if I'd driven off that bridge tonight, or turned it over on a bad curve, but to know I died in the cab while I was parked, and she not knowing what killed me. Poor Sarah, I wish I could have told her.*

He was prepared to witness his death, but he was curious to know what it was going to be like where he was going, or if he were to continue living, what it would be like, being a vegetable for how may untold years? He wondered, *Would he know he was a vegetable? Would he be aware of people around him?* Then, he thought about Sarah again. *Would he know who she was when she came to visit him?* That thought transfixed his madness for a burning moment and gave him one last hope. *Why not call her? Call her not to say goodbye, but to see if she might help him tonight. Maybe there's something she would say that would bring him back from the cliff he was about to tumble over. But he didn't want to scare her or put her through worry or strain. No, he wouldn't do that.* He thought about it for several minutes. *Who, if anyone, should he call and ask for help? It had to be Sarah. No one else would understand. God, how he loved her! So, if I do call her, what exactly do I say? That I'm dying and here will be the location of my body when the sun comes up. No. I can't do that. Why don't I just tell her the truth? I'm having a nervous breakdown, and I need to be hospitalized immediately. Please get on a plane and get up here and manage things.* He was on to something now, a way out of the horror. Sarah and a hospital. The more he thought about it the better it sounded. He picked up his cell phone and started to push the pre-select for his home in Alabama. He wanted to do it; he wanted to call her. Then he thought, *No, I should call the police or hospital first. Have them come get me first, then call Sarah.* He also knew that a third call would be required – a call to Mountaintop Transport. Then it dawned on him. If that were the outcome, that he called Mountaintop Transport and explained to them he had admitted himself to a hospital and abandoned his truck, then he would also have to abandon his plans for the fourth decision. Even as bad off as he was tonight, he didn't think he could do that.

He dressed for the cold and climbed out of the truck and headed off through the woods. The snow had stopped. It was now raining. By the time he had trudged ten minutes into the woods he was soaked to the bone. He sat down against a tree and listened to the rain for a long time. Then he started praying.

Chapter Twelve

Mountaintop Transport had run him up and down the East Coast two times after that very bad night in New York and Pennsylvania. They also had dispatched him back into New York City, but Toby refused to go. Evidently they valued keeping him as a driver who would no longer make New York City trips more than they valued him as an ex-driver. He'd been mostly in the south running deliveries for a major retailer in South Carolina, Georgia, and Florida.

Ever since that bad night, Toby had lived up to his new resolution of working on the fourth decision a minimum of two hours a day. He would fire up his computer every night before he turned in and locate web sites to find the information he needed. His potential target list was narrowing down to something manageable. Now, he was really beginning to focus on the delivery system, his truck, and the bomb itself. He recalled the night Coon Dog had described the steps that a bomb maker would have to take if he were to duplicate what Tim McVeigh had pulled off. Ammonia nitrate? No problem. The farmers around Lake Thomas use it all the time. Why, he even used it himself at the golf course. He'd been gathering the ammonium nitrate in an empty corner of his barn on his two and three day home stints. As a matter of fact, it was beginning to worry him a bit. What if someone started getting suspicious? No, he thought, nobody would catch on. There was no reason for the police or Feds to look in his barn. He figured that very soon he'd be prepared to act on the fourth decision. He also figured that the Billy Waynick problem would be over soon.

A week later, somewhere in Georgia, Toby again picked up the paperback novel that had been untouched in his sleeper for over a month. During that time he had often thought about the story but hadn't had the energy or time to read. Now, he hoped he'd find out what happened to Windjammer and Bryant Harrison on that giant wave.

* * *

When Windjammer felt the skeg ram the tail of Harrison's board, he went hurtling and skipping across the wave like a flat rock thrown across a country pond. He flipped a couple of times and had no chance at all to orient himself or take any deep breathes. Then eighty tons of Pacific Ocean came down on him. Harrison, after he'd been kicked around to the right by the force of Jammer's skeg, quickly made another mistake. He flipped the board over on top of himself and hung on for dear life seeking protection. When the wave slammed down on him, the surf board exploded into ten or twelve pieces. So much for the protection he sought. Both surfers were driven to the bottom and raked over the coral and the lava rock. Harrison was nearly pinned in the sand between two lava rocks. It actually helped him get oriented to know which way was up. Windjammer did not fare as well. As he was pounded and rolled around on the bottom he was not able to determine which way to the surface, nearly twenty-six feet above.

On the beach the word spread quickly. Windjammer and Harrison collided on a thirty-eight footer. Everyone, Natalie included, looked to those with the telephoto cameras and the field glasses and pleaded anxiously, "Can you see them, yet? Have they come up yet?"

Richard Loeffler had his field glasses roughly on the area where the two were swallowed up and was panning the snarling, foaming surface but could not detect anything or anyone bobbing up.

The young local was really worried now, "Dee haoles still down on dee bottom," he shouted. "Don't know if dey goin' to make it."

The old Hawaiian kahuna was still deep in his chant, actually a trance-like state, and he couldn't hear any of the shouting and hysteria going on around him.

It had been forty seconds since the unbelievable wipeout had thrown them on the bottom. Harrison was nearing the surface and would break it in another ten seconds. Jammer, still disoriented and suffering a concussion was in big trouble. He wasn't able to get good air in his lungs when he went under, and now those lungs were burning, and he was getting light headed as well. For a second he thought it was an incoming mortar round that got him, and he instinctively went for his k-bar to fend off the gook he saw preparing to bayonet him. *Damn the First Sergeant! I told him we never should of gone into that ville.* But as he grabbed for his k-bar he had nothing but water. *Oh no! I'm surely going to go down on this one.* And then he faded quickly and was ready to cash in his chips. He had one last thought. It was about Ron Willis. *There was something I was going to do. What was it? I can't go yet. Can't die now. There's something that must be done. Ron Willis, Ron Willis, what was it?* Then he remembered Richard Loeffler. Now he was fighting to stay conscious, to stay alive. He was flailing away at the water but still couldn't get a direction for up. His eyes were open and burning, but there was nothing but gray and blue and quivering metallic shafts of light, but from what direction he could not tell.

The old Hawaiian's trance and chant had drained him totally, but still he went to the ocean spirit brothers and sought their aide for Windjammer.

Harrison had cleared the surface and was sucking in good air and looking for any remnant of his board. On the bottom Windjammer began to fade again. Then through the swirling salt and sand and the eerie grayish-blue foggy light he saw the image of a Manta Ray coming his way through the turbulence. It was coming for him. He knew instantly it was coming to his aide. He felt Mother Ocean smile, and he fought with all he had to follow the ray. It led him up, up, up.

Loeffler's field glasses settled in on a solitary head bobbing in the wake of the number three wave. "One of them is up," he shouted. A roar from the crowd rang from the beach to the palm trees, all the way back to Kam Highway. Loeffler raised the angle of his field glasses to see if he had missed anything bobbing up further out. He didn't see the second surfer that he was searching for. Instead he did see the number four wave of the set swelling up and rumbling towards the beach, a mile away. Loeffler shifted back to where he'd seen someone bobbing, and this time he spotted two heads bobbing up and down in the ocean. They were obviously aware of each others presence as they were only maybe twenty feet apart.

"They're both up!" shouted Loeffler. Another roar echoed up and down the beach, this one louder than the first. Natalie and the group she was with allowed some high fives and some cautious optimism. They were aware that these two guys were still in plenty of danger.

As soon as Windjammer had broken the surface and gulped in as much air as he could, it was as if his fading mental capacity, grogginess, and nearly unconscious state had simply disappeared. It might have been purely survival instinct. It might have been his brother ocean spirits were taking over. What ever it was, he instantly assessed the situation he was in, yet another moment of truth, and made another split second decision. This time he wasn't going to let Harrison make any more mistakes. He screamed over at him, "Hey you! Follow me!" Then he swam viciously to the take off spot in order to body surf number four.

Harrison was right with him. They got to the spot, turned and swam hard, even more viciously, towards the beach. Somehow they got a shift in the wind; just enough of an off shore gust to hold number four up a few seconds longer. The old Hawaiian was coming out of his trance and the beginnings of a big smile started sneaking across the corners of his mouth. Windjammer and Bryant Harrison dropped down the face of the number four wave. They were skimming along on their chest and torso at thirty miles per hour. Number four turned out to be a paltry twenty-five footer, but it's story became legendary on Oahu's North Shore. Most say there never was or will be another tube hollowed out like number four was that day. The fact that the two surfers inside it were cutting circular wakes in and out of each others path, that they were spinning and doing body flops inside that wave; nobody could ever recall such an event!

By the time the wave had given up all its energy to the inside soup, there were two other surfers there to share their boards with Windjammer and Harrison. A few minutes later all four were coming in on the shore break. Natalie was the first to come to Windjammer, and a throng gathered around Bryant Harrison.

Many in the beach crowd, especially the surf photographers and cameramen tried to get Windjammer to talk about what it was like to wipe out on a thirty-eight foot wave. He didn't say much, just that he was glad no one was hurt. He seemed pre-occupied. There was definitely something on his mind. A few minutes later he spotted Loeffler. He told Natalie he'd be back in a minute.

They had walked down the beach a short way, "What happened to Ron Willis?"

The question surprised Loeffler but there was no evidence of it on his face or in his body language. Years of lying, half truths, all kinds of treachery and black ops would easily insulate him from such a meager interrogation.

"There were some circumstances beyond my control that were responsible for that unfortunate situation."

Windjammer considered that and looked Loeffler straight in the eyes, "You can save all that phony spook double talk. What happened? Did you forget to do your homework? Everybody knows the Pake's from downtown run all the growing operations on the Windward side. You of all people should have known that. You did know that! Then you suckered in a good marine to go out there and take the fall. Ron wasn't perfect. He had his problems, but he didn't deserve what you did to him."

* * *

Chapter Thirteen

It was early morning light in Kansas. Toby had been driving since a half hour before sun-up. He knew that today, as he made his way towards Denver, he would stop several times just to walk out a ways on the flat prairie and let the cold wind leak through his clothes. The day was uneventful, and he didn't anticipate any problems finding a parking place just inside the Colorado line. There were numerous places to park including one of his favorite truck stops. The place really had a western prairie feel to it. He was still an hour away, and this Kansas portion of planet Earth was spinning away from the sun, creating the magnificent sunset and then the night.

Toby had been chattering on the CB trying to sound like an old hand at the jabber that passed for real conversation. It was better than the worn out tapes and CDs he got tired of listening to. Even the right wing talk radio that he was tuned in to much of the time on the satellite sometimes would bore him. He must have heard ten dirty jokes on the CB in the last hour. Also, truckers weren't reluctant to trade jabs with each other about wives and girlfriends. A few minutes ago Toby heard a trucker tell another that the other trucker's wife was probably so fat that he spent all his money trying to feed her. The other trucker came back and said, "No, not really. Dog food don't cost much."

It also wouldn't take long to find an ass-whoopin' conversation on the CB. Usually a wise crack about another driver's manhood was all that was needed to get it started. A lot of drivers kept a spare can of 'Whoop-Ass' in their truck and were always ready to open it and use it. Ninety-nine times out of a hundred the use was verbal. Occasionally, a real fight would take place, and somebody would get hurt.

Toby had been talking with another driver about the weather around Denver tomorrow. He put the mike back on its catch and was reaching for his water bottle when he heard that unmistakable, strong, Appalachian voice of Moses incarnate come across the CB. "Break one nine. This is the Christian Truck Driver's Ministry. Good evening drivers. I surely do hope and pray that the Good Lord is providing you with a special blessing tonight. Drivers, won't you please drop down to channel 7 for prayer and fellowship." Toby went to channel 7 but told himself he would only listen in.

The man prayed in a similar way to what Toby had heard the last time. It was just as strong and mesmerizing tonight as it was then. Just like the last time there were several 'amen's from other drivers. One driver started telling the new world Moses, as Toby thought of him, about all the personal and family problems he was having. The CB Christian spiritual man answered with a touching and gripping prayer for the driver who responded with, "Thank you preacher! Thank you preacher! That means a lot to me."

Then a few minutes later another driver came on the CB airwaves. "Preacher, would you sing us that truck drivin' song I heard you a singin' down in South Carolina a month ago?"

"Well, I ain't sung it in awhile, but I'll do my best." Toby was still listening as the man started out on a melody that might have come from the deepest, darkest holler in all Appalachia, and it also came from the deepest part of any man Toby had ever heard sing any song.

Open highway, Open Highway I hear your call.
Like an angry old lover, you wanted my all.
Well, I'll give you what I got, but it ain't
very much.
Jesus my Savior, now He's my real crutch.

Now I started truck drivin' to see if I could.
Now I'm driving forever, I knew that I would.
Open highway, open highway, you've tortured
my soul.
You've run me through this land, so that's
where I'll go.

Yes, I'll die on your pavement, and if they will fit,
My brakes and my drive shaft, right there they
will sit.
But my soul's going to heaven, not to your
big road.
Jesus my Savior will carry my load.

Now they say that truck drivers are modern
cowboys.
They lead a rough life, but that is their choice.
And they say that the cowboys all ride to be free.
And truck drivers are sailors on that big
concrete sea.

Now truck drivers and cowboys they like to roam.
But only dear Jesus can show their way home.
Yes only dear Jesus can show their way home.

You had the feeling that living in and driving a truck was the actual blood flowing through the singer's veins. Toby conjured up an image of a hard living, wise, weather-beaten man behind the wheel of that truck, and he knew he was going to talk to him. "Preacher, you got any more songs like that?"

"Hello, Toby. I was wonderin' when we'd meet up again."

This time Toby wasn't surprised by the driver's response. "Did you know I was coming, like the last time?"

"Not exactly. I think I knew you were in the area. But I didn't know we were going to meet up. I'm feeling like you had more to do with it than I did."

Toby thought about that and said, "Yes, maybe that's true. Are you westbound? Maybe we could get a cup of coffee?"

Toby's mental image of a leather faced, hard living man was accurate enough but didn't do justice to Jabez's sparkling hazel eyes. When they caught you they could hold you, and that voice, it was even more powerful and disarming in person. They were in the Burlington, Colorado Truck Stop and Café. Toby liked it because the people were friendly and the food was much better than most truck stop food. The place had a good feel to it. They had sat down a minute ago. The waitress was returning with their coffee.

"They call me Jabez. My real name is Pete Thompson. It doesn't make any difference, you know. I think where the bible says 'He knows us by name', He has His own name for us."

"Jabez, that's a bible name isn't it?" Toby said.

"Yes, it is. How long have you been drivin' trucks?"

Toby was stirring his coffee to cool it. "I've only been driving maybe four and a half months. How long have you been driving?"

Jabez was stirring his coffee too, "Aw, round thirty five years I reckon."

"I guess you've seen a lot of changes since you first started," Toby said.

"Yeah, probably more than I could count, but you know some things never change. You got some good people out here drivin', and then you got some not so good people. That hasn't changed at all. Tell me why you started drivin'."

Toby was drinking his coffee now, and he took his time, "Well, I just needed a change. I wasn't very happy doing what I was doing. I thought about several other kinds of work I might try, but I finally decided on truck driving."

Jabez pierced him with those powerful hazel eyes, and Toby knew he had been caught lying. Jabez didn't have to say anything. They both knew it.

"Okay. Let's just say there were certain events that took place, and I, uh, well, I thought truck driving might fit in and kind of go along with my planning."

"What kind of planning are you doing?" Those eyes were going through Toby again.

"Oh, it's kind of personal. I haven't even shared it with my wife. I want it to be a surprise."

Jabez put his coffee cup down, "Does it have something to do with the thing you were struggling with that night back in Virginia?"

Surprisingly, Jabez's questions weren't getting Toby angry. Toby just reasoned that Jabez was simply being true to his nature. He seemed to be legitimately concerned about people. Toby would skirt the truth about what his real plans were as long as necessary. He had no intentions of telling anybody about them.

"No, no, my plans have nothing to do with that," Toby said. Jabez didn't badger Toby. They both ordered a meal and talked. Toby learned a lot about Pete Thompson. His CB handle, Jabez, was from First Chronicles, chapter four, verses nine and ten. Most truck driver's CB handles come from the drivers themselves. The assumption that CB handles are nicknames attached to them by other drivers is usually incorrect. Pete loved the "Prayer of Jabez" recorded in the Chronicles scripture, so tagged himself Jabez on the CB. Pete told Toby that the prayer has been a guiding light for him. Its simplicity and direct request for blessings, Pete said, can't be found any other place in the Bible:

"And Jabez called on the God of Israel saying,
Oh, that You would bless me indeed,
And enlarge my territory,
That Your hand would be with me,
And that You would keep me from evil,
That I may not cause pain!
So God granted him what he requested."

Toby had listened carefully as Jabez had recited the prayer, "Where did you say that prayer is from?"

"The book of First Chronicles in the Old Testament," Jabez said.

"You're right. That is simple, but powerful." Toby wondered about this old truck driver he was talking with. *What gave him that special, genuine spirituality that was impossible not to see? Where did the power to discover, perceive, divine, comprehend or whatever it was he did, a complete stranger's name come from. How about his ability to read another person's mind? Where did that come from?* "Jabez, you said back in Virginia that you get visions, or, I think you said, premonitions. Would I be correct in guessing they come from God?"

"Yes. I've had the gift for a long time. You know, the Heavenly Father communicates with us in lots of different ways. Some of His chosen have certain abilities. I call them gifts. Ever since I was a young lad, I've wanted to know if I had the chance to be one of His chosen. I wanted to. I wanted to reign with Him in the New Jerusalem."

Toby beckoned the waitress for more coffee. "Were you able to see things when you were young? You know, visions, premonitions?"

"I remember when I was a boy; we lived way back in the mountains. There was a creek I'd fish in and play in. One day I was lying on the bank of the creek lookin' up into the sky, and I saw flying saucers just a scootin' across the sky. Some were three to a squadron, some were more. They just kept comin', all of them flying across the sky. I watched it for hours and hours and finally before dark I went on home. That was before all the technology of today. People today are caught up in so much deceit, nonsense, sin, war, and hate they don't take time to look for God. God is continually giving us signs and directives. He put it all down in 'The Book'. Those flying saucers I saw as a boy, that's nothing. We are so caught up in worldly ways and things, we fail to see the big picture. In this humongous cosmos called eternity we are among the most primitive. There are others. They are watching us." Jabez stopped to drink more of his coffee.

Toby said, "I've seen things in the night skies. I guess most people would think I'm crazy."

"No, Toby, you're not crazy. When I met you out in the parking lot, I of course knew from that night in Virginia you've been struggling with something, and tonight I know there's been another problem come along since then. I don't know what either of these things is, but they do exist. I know that. But tonight when I met you I sensed a Godly nature in you. You see, some of us have spiritual antennae. When my antenna is turned on, and I think it is turned on most of the time, I don't really know how that works. I can sense the aura that people give off. I can read whether they give off good and Godly energy, or whether they give off evil energy. You, my friend, are a man who gives off Godly energy. You aren't crazy."

If only this man knew my real nature, my truck bomb plans, my plans for Billy Waynick. I bet then he wouldn't be calling me godly, Toby thought. But, he realized that Jabez probably would have continued to pray for him, anyway.

That night in the Burlington Colorado Truck Stop and Café, Toby listened to Jabez tell of his visions of a heavenly city, streets of gold and silver. There were columns, eight feet wide, going up, and up, and up. Jabez couldn't see the tops, but he did see a huge figure in a hooded, floor length, silver cape. Jabez said he couldn't see any facial features, but he felt like he was in the presence of God. Jabez told Toby that one day as a young man, he was on that same creek he grew up on. He was in prayer and meditation and prayed, "Lord, I wish you would show me something of beauty this morning." He looked down near the creek and saw the most beautiful white lily growing in the sand where he had left a footprint.

That night Pete Thompson went back to his truck to get a few hours sleep. He would be up before the sun and halfway to Wyoming. Toby wondered what kind of truck driving song Pete and God would be singing together when the first rays of golden sunlight reflected off Pete's truck. In a way Toby envied Jabez's demeanor and spirit. He wondered if he would ever get to a similar place. He realized he had some thinking and praying to do.

Chapter Fourteen

Toby was on his way back to Alabama. He was glad he had run into Jabez. He had met several drivers that he respected and liked in his short driving career, but Jabez had made him re-examine his own spiritual side. More than that, Toby was now forced to look at himself in the mirror. He and Jabez had talked for hours, and more than once Jabez had referred to the fact that there were good drivers out there and not so good. It didn't take Toby long to understand that the conversation had nothing to do with the drivers actual skill at handling a big rig but rather was a statement about the nature of a driver's soul.

When Toby began to consider the nature of his own soul, he didn't like what he saw, so he stopped looking. Instead, he intensified his planning on the fourth decision and his thinking on what to do about Billy Waynick.

Billy Waynick's new job at Tyler Red Flag Advertising, in Birmingham, had been coming along very nicely, Billy thought. After his encounter with Carolyn Etheridge and Ronnie Matlock on the golf course back in September, Billy had taken an impromptu vacation to the Caribbean and upon his return, he quickly submitted his two week notice to the advisory board at the golf course. Billy's new employer, Sanford T. Littlejohn, had owned the Tyler Red Flag Advertising Agency for five years. Sanford knew about and had no compunctions about Billy's sexual proclivities.

In fact the two had enjoyed several sexually perverted encounters together. Privately when they were in each others company, they referred to themselves as 'Sans Baby', and 'Billy Bunny'.

Billy usually left his house around eight o'clock in the morning and arrived at work forty-five minutes later. Although Billy had moved closer to Birmingham, he maintained a home a good ways back in the woods just as he had done in Lake Thomas. The driveway was secluded by deep woods before it opened to a clearing where Billy's four hundred thousand dollar house, complete with cabana, pool and other play areas, was situated. This morning Billy's quarter mile entrance driveway to his home was blocked by several large logs. As Billy noticed the logs blocking his exit and as he came to a stop, his eyes instinctively looked up to his rearview mirror. He froze. He saw Toby Etheridge emerge from the woods on his side with a twelve gauge shotgun leveled at his head.

"Roll the window down," Toby instructed Billy.

Frightened, but knowing that there was no other option, Billy found the switch and opened the window all the way. He said, "Toby, w-what are you doing? W-what's g-going on? I-I can... Look. I c-can ex-explain every... I can explain e-everything." He was stuttering, and he began to feel wetness in his pants.

"Get out," Toby ordered him.

"Toby. No! No! You can't do this!"

"Shut up and get out!" Toby was about eight feet away from Billy. The twelve gauge was aimed squarely at Billy's head.

Billy fumbled at the door handle, opened it and tried to step out, but his legs gave way, and he slumped to his knees on the ground, his arms holding onto the open door for support.

"Get up," Toby ordered him.

Billy stumbled to his feet, closed the door, and leaned on the side of the car for support.

"Okay, now I want you to do what I say. Do you understand?"

"Yeah." Resignation was heavy in Billy's voice.

"Okay, I'm going to ask you one question. You've got one chance here. Do you understand?"

"What do you mean, I've got one chance?"

Speaking each word slowly and with emphasis, Toby replied, "Exactly what I said. You've got one chance here. I'm going to ask you the question, and then you've got one chance to give me the answer."

"You mean I've only got one chance to give you the right answer? Is that what you mean?" Billy's mind was a blur. He was trying to figure which way to go. Tell the truth or cover up. But he could not read Toby, what direction the question might go, and more importantly, what kind of answer could he come up with that might satisfy him. "Toby, look, I'm not sure I understand."

Toby cut him off with a ferocity a pit bull might show a stray cat, "Alright! Shut up! Enough!" Then melodramatically toning down the volume and hatred, "Here's the question. Do you know why I'm here, with a gun aimed at your head?" Toby was burning a hole through Billy's head with his eyes.

Billy was at a total loss as to how to answer. He figured that if he said yes, he was sure to die, and if he said no, well, maybe that would stall things. He thought it over. Toby seemed to be in no hurry now that the question had been asked, but he showed no signs of backing the twelve gauge off, or of turning down the intensity of his eyes. Billy took more time and finally decided on his answer but held it as long as he could.

"Okay, let's have it." Toby said.

"Well, I , uh, I. No, I don't know why you are here." Billy barely managed to get it out.

Toby continued looking through Billy, "Now listen closely and do exactly as I say. You understand?"

Billy could only nod his head. He would not say another word.

"Get back in the car."

Billy got in and closed the door.

"Back it up right over there." Toby pointed to a weedy patch between the driveway and the woods. Toby was walking along side, the shotgun still leveled at Billy's head.

Billy put the car where Toby wanted it, stopping about ten feet from the edge of the woods.

"Pop the trunk open."

Billy found the switch and did so.

"Now, get out," Toby waved the 12 gauge at him. "Walk back there," Toby motioned Billy to the edge of the woods. "You know, if you had told me the truth, this wouldn't be happening. I was going to let you go. Do you want to say a prayer?"

Billy's tears were tumbling down his cheeks, but he was incapable of prayer or words.

"You know, I heard a prayer the other day you should have been praying a long time ago."

"And Jabez called on the God of Israel saying,

'Oh, that You would bless me indeed,

And enlarge my territory,

That Your hand would be with me,

And that You would keep me from evil,

That I may not cause pain!'

So God granted him what he requested."

Then Toby fired.

That night Toby slipped in the back door to his house hoping no one would be up and stirring, but he heard the TV in the den. He looked in and found Sarah, Carolyn, and Derrick. "Hi, honey, I thought you'd get in earlier," Sarah said. No one got up or seemed to divert their attention from the TV.

Good, Toby thought. He didn't feel like talking to anyone. He grabbed a snack then sat with his family. In his mind, he was going over the day's events, reviewing his cleanup activities at Billy Waynick's, trying to determine if he'd missed something or made any mistakes that would land him in prison or subject himself to Alabama's electric chair.

The next day Toby stayed busy on his preparations for the fourth decision. It was Friday. Sarah was working, and Carolyn and Derrick were both in school. Today was the day – the day he would assemble the ammonium nitrate fuel oil bomb in the back of his empty trailer. He had been stockpiling the fertilizer in a corner of his barn. It had not been difficult for Toby to lie to local farmers about his need to buy a small amount from them. The golf course was using it and Toby was simply helping out the new man that replaced him. Little did the farmers know that the small amounts they sold to Toby ended up in his barn, not at the golf course, or that in three months Toby's cumulative purchases of ammonium nitrate amounted to nearly six tons. The barrels of fuel oil were also easy for Toby to acquire. As for the cell phone activated detonator, Toby had acquired what he needed in less than three weeks. Several specialty electronic companies had the components, and Toby was able to assemble the detonator and even test a prototype to his satisfaction.

Before loading and assembling the materials for the bomb inside the trailer, he put the finishing touches on the 'drop mechanisms' he had devised in order to be able to quickly disengage the trailer from the tractor without exiting the cab. Toby had cut a hole in the back wall of the cab and mounted a steel guide support on the left of the twin beam frame just under the fifth wheel. He inserted a ten foot long steel rod through the hole and through a two inch circular eye hook which was mounted on the guide support. The outside end of the steel rod was hooked so that when the rod was turned and manipulated it would catch the fifth wheel release handle. On the inside of the tractor the steel rod passed through a four inch eye hook which was mounted to the floor of the cab. The contraption allowed Toby to effectively release the locking arm on the fifth wheel of the trailer's king pin from the drivers seat. All Toby had to do was reach down, rotate the rod ninety degrees, lever it upwards on the eye hooks, then lever it away from him with a hard jerk. He could detach the trailer from the tractor while moving down the road or from a stop, never leaving the drivers seat.

He had cut another hole through the back wall of the cab in order to disengage the electrical pigtail and the two airlines from the trailer, again without exiting the cab. He had fashioned a special harness for these three lines and replaced the old one with his new one. Again he had a steel rod mounted through the hole which allowed him to very easily and quickly disengage the trailers three support lines without getting out of the driver's seat. He tested both devises over and over. They worked flawlessly.

As he worked he wondered about this new creature he was becoming. He had felt very little emotion yesterday or today about Billy Waynick. He remembered that a few years back he had cried after he had to put one of his dogs down. When he buried it, he put one of his shirts in the grave under the dog's head. He was upset for days, and still, now, it was difficult to think about it. Billy Waynick, on the other hand, seemingly affected him no more than if it had been a poison snake's head he'd cut off. He'd killed many of them around his farm and on the golf course, and although the killing had to be done, he didn't like seeing the snakes in their squirming, slithering death dance. How would he feel if he was successful on his fourth decision? What about the Muslim fanatics he was about to kill? He was planning on sending hundreds to Allah. Every time he thought about it, all he could see in his mind's eye were the nightmarish images of 9-11 and the Twin Towers burning and tumbling down. Would he ever be able to sequence those two numbers, nine and eleven, and not see those horrible, unstoppable images, not see the bodies falling from the sky?

By mid-afternoon Toby had completed the loading, assembling, and final preparations of all components of a massive ammonium nitrate fuel oil truck bomb. In 1995

Timothy McVeigh used four thousand, eight hundred pounds of ammonium nitrate to blow up the Oklahoma City Federal Building, killing 168 people. Toby Etheridge had nearly three times that amount.

The next morning, Saturday morning, Toby rolled over close to Sarah with a sexual urgency that would not be denied. Afterwards Toby thought what a lucky man he was. A woman like Sarah didn't just come along everyday. He often told his friends that he and Sarah weren't responsible for the solid marriage they enjoyed, but that all the credit went to God. Toby and Sarah never forgot their marriage vows or the way the preacher described marriage as a holy union, a union consecrated by God. Of all the questionable things Toby Etheridge was, or was about to become, a man with an unloving heart and disloyalty to his wife were not two of those things. Toby knew that if things went badly the next few days, he and Sarah may never again share another session of love making, and he tried to put the thought out of his mind. He was also mindful that if things went badly, he may not even return home, and the thoughts of not being with Carolyn and Derrick again implored him to reconsider his plans for the fourth decision – but not for long. The burning desire to 'do something' in retaliation for the 9-11 attacks was overwhelming. And, now that the bomb had been built, and a final decision on which target to attack had been made as well. The only thing left to do was to drive his truck to the target and carry out his mission – KAMTAP. Surely God would be with him and bring him home safely. He had convinced himself that surely this thing he was about to do was in fact God's will. He did not realize that his rationale was the same as the enemy's.

Toby spent most of the day with Sarah, Carolyn, and Derrick. Toby had insisted that they go down by the lake for a picnic, and they went along with his request. They had done this many times as a family. In Alabama a seventy degree day was not unusual in the dead of winter. Later that afternoon, after the picnic Toby drove his pick-up to Coon Dog's. Coon Dog was in the shed working on some homemade flies he would use in some trout streams up in the mountains. Coon Dog's coffee was laced with Bourbon, but Toby poured himself a cup of pure black "When you going to the mountains?" Toby asked him.

"Probably Wednesday. I'm guiding for some fellers from New Orleans that want to do some trout fishing."

"You remember those girls we took fishin' back in the tenth grade?"

A smile came to Coon Dog's face. "I sure do. As I recall, you did a little guided tour of your own on Peggy Clarkson's torso."

"You remember that? I'll tell you what, she was way too classy to be messing around with me."

Coon Dog raised his eyebrows and slightly shook his head, "Really? Then why did you two continue dating for the next two years?"

"Oh hell, I don't remember." Toby was lying. The truth was that Peggy had meant a lot to Toby. He had told her he wanted to marry her, and although she never really truly said yes, she never said no either. Toby went in the Navy right after high school, and a year later when his ship steamed across the Pacific to Vietnam, Peggy quit writing. He never saw her again.

Coon Dog wondered about the reason for Toby's visit. Was he here to pry him for more on what happened on the golf course back in September, or maybe to get more information on bombs and explosives. It must be something along those lines. Toby wasn't in the habit of dropping by for small talk. That's what Coon Dog did. But Toby seemed to be in a melancholy mood, and he kept asking Coon Dog if he remembered things from the fifties and sixties. Toby asked him if he remembered the nights their families would all be together on the big front porch on summer nights at Toby's grandparent's house. They'd talk and talk. Most of the men were smoking Lucky Strikes or Camels, or chewing Mail Pouch or Redman, and Uncle Henry always had his pipe lit up. The little ones would be out in the yard catching lightning bugs. Everyone enjoyed the hunting and fishing stories exchanged by the men. Coon Dog's daddy, Horace, told the best stories and never failed to get everybody laughing.

Toby went on and on with the memories. Coon Dog added some, and before they knew it, two hours had gone by. Toby stood to leave and said, "It's a different world now. It all changed in the sixties. Vietnam changed a lot of things for sure. The drugs, the sex, all the rebellion changed things too. Your grandparents, your mom and dad, my grandparents, all the old timers; we'll never see days like that again, will we?"

"No. I reckon not," Coon Dog said.

"Coon Dog, that night I called you, the night I was on the road, you know, I asked you about Carolyn and that day at the golf course. Well, I won't ever be asking you about it again. You understand what I'm saying?"

"Yeah, Toby, I understand."

* * *

Sunday morning, 4:30 a.m., Toby Etheridge slipped quietly out of bed, made coffee to fill his thermos, and then climbed up in the cab of his eighteen wheeler. He had enough food, water, and supplies to last him for weeks. He also had his deer rifle, his twelve gauge, and a .38 caliber automatic pistol on board. He had enough ammunition to hold off a good sized posse. He started the motor and while it was warming up he double checked everything inside the trailer, then put two padlocks on the closed trailer doors. Next, he did a thorough inspection of his tires and lights. Finally, he punched in the code on the qual-com satellite computer to verify the load of auto parts he was to pick up in Columbus, Georgia. It was scheduled to be loaded into his trailer at 8:00 a.m. The parts were going to Detroit, Michigan.

He was wound up pretty tight, excited and nervous. He realized he loved the feeling of settling in behind the wheel when a new trip started. There was just something that felt good about firing up a big truck that you control totally. The four hundred seventy five horsepower monster reacted only to you. You controlled everything that would happen in that truck for the next few days. You also would control pretty much everything that happened around your truck. Day after day Toby listened to truck drivers on the CB complaining about four wheelers getting in their way, cutting them off, camping out right in front of them, etc. As Toby saw it, it was just the opposite. His sense was that when he came through an intersection, or was entering an interstate via the on-ramp, the four wheelers gave him a wide berth. They were definitely aware of his presence. He liked that feeling. He didn't go out of his way to flaunt his truck's size and power, but he didn't shy away from situations either. He looked around him, all the lights flickering on the dash, the radios, and the computers.

Red lights, green lights, yellow lights, and others. And the smell, he sure liked it. It was a combination of grease, diesel fuel, body odor, air freshener, and Armor All. Somehow the mix of it all was something you could only smell in a big truck cab. Sarah had said the smell nauseated her, but not Toby. He liked it. All of these things were a comfort to him this morning. They were home, and he was going into uncharted territory. This trip would certainly change his life in ways he couldn't begin to fathom.

Before arriving at the auto parts shipping dock, Toby pulled into a Mountaintop Transport drop yard, some eighteen miles from the shipper. Most large truck companies maintained drop yards at scattered locations around the United States. Their purpose was to serve as a holding area for both empty and loaded trailers. Many of these drop yards were manned by a single security guard at the gate, who would only log the tractor and trailer numbers of units going in and out of the yard. Others were not manned at all. In that case there was usually an electronic gate that a driver could open with a code punched in on the keypad posted outside the gate. Such was the case where Toby was this morning.

He opened the gate, drove in, and commenced to search the four rows of trailers for an empty that looked as close as possible to his bomb loaded trailer. He selected a fifty-three foot Great Dane with the same company logo on it as his. He got out and checked it out to make sure the auto parts shipper would give it a green light to have their product shipped in. He then quickly spray painted over the trailer's five digit I.D. number on the nose and tail of the trailer. Then Toby backed the bomb trailer into a nearby empty hole, dropped it, and pulled his tractor up under the empty until he heard and felt the fifth wheel locking arm attach to the kingpin securely. He waited as long as he could to give the spray paint more time to dry to a satisfactory level, then he placed his template over the almost completely dry areas where the empty trailers I.D. numbers had been. He sprayed over the template with black paint, pulled the template off, and now the empty trailer had the same number as the bomb trailer. Again he allowed as much time as he could to let the paint dry, then he exited the drop yard, and made his way to the auto parts shipping dock.

Things went smoothly at the shipping dock. His empty trailer with the correct I.D. number spray painted on it, was loaded in about forty- five minutes. Toby signed the shipping papers. Then he drove back to the drop yard and dropped the trailer loaded with auto parts. He then hooked back up to the trailer loaded with death. He double checked the route he would use, and aimed his truck north towards Detroit, Michigan. For a rookie truck driver he wasn't doing badly. That is, if you were counting the laws he was breaking and would continue to break. In that regard, he was setting records.

In the Muslim world an Imam is the officiating priest of a mosque. Imam, Siraj Rashid, was describing the preparations that had been made for tomorrow's annual North American Conference of Islamic Leaders at one of the many mosques in Dearborn, about ten miles from downtown Detroit. He and his fellow conference members were having a working lunch at a Muslim restaurant. There were fifteen to twenty conference members in attendance and everyone it seemed was anxious to get the three day conference convened on schedule tomorrow at noon. They all agreed that there were many pressing issues that needed to be addressed, not the least of which was the actual physical security of mosques throughout the United States. Many threats of attacks had been reported since 9-11, and in two southern states police had barely enough warning to stop two attacks that had appeared eminent.

Rashid glanced down at his notes and continued, "Our esteemed and honorable senior Imam here in Detroit, Abdul Rahman, tells me that tomorrow's opening meeting will be surrounded by perhaps five hundred local Muslims who have declared that they feel they must be in attendance on opening day in order to participate in the Iqamah to Allah for the success of our conference. Naturally, we preferred a less conspicuous start to the conference, in that security is a legitimate concern. You are of course aware that our conference has received considerable coverage in at least the regional press. Since our brother Muslims are insistent on being here tomorrow, we will honor their desire to join us in Iqamah."

Toby made it well into Ohio by Sunday night. He stopped at an interstate rest area where he was lucky enough to find a vacant parking spot. Everything today had worked smoothly. In fact, the day's activities seemed a bit anticlimactic. He had given so much thought beforehand, figuring any and all contingencies, that the real preparation had all floated by as if it were all a dream.

When he dropped off into a fitful sleep, it was as if it were a dream within a dream. He saw Coon Dog and himself dressed in fatigues. They were in the Mekong Delta on a swift boat taking small arms fire, not from the shoreline, but from somewhere under the Earth's surface. The rounds erupted from the river around them and tore up through the boat's decks. There were women on the shoreline laughing at everything. The women were not native Vietnamese. They were beautiful round eyed women with flowing green moss strands lazily hanging from limbs and torso. Some breasts were semi covered with the sultry moss; some were fully exposed. In his mind's eye he watched them transform as the moss and limbs grew to cover the women as if they were wearing a burqah. He sensed the women were not laughing at him or Coon Dog but were joyously shrieking, reveling about their Muslim men who were soon to receive them as part of Allah's seventy virgin reward. Immediately Toby's dream took on the speed of a photo show, slide by slide. He was both in front of the camera and directing it. Images flashed all around him. He had a sense of a battle. He could sense gunfire and exploding concrete. He could see the role models of his youth, his little league coach, the milk driver, farmer Brown sitting on his tractor. *Were these warriors, too?* From the river's edge VC were threatening them. Then it seemed each photo froze, becoming a two dimensional reality. Each particle started coming apart. He could hear the women's cackle, the gunfire, splashing water, crumbling buildings, and a symphony of cries as all matter was reduced to neutron level. The sense of it was that each neutron weighed a trillion tons and was marching through Toby's head. *Why did each molecule seem so horrendously heavy?* The night wore on. Real sleep never came. Just dreams inside of nightmares.

By ten o'clock Monday morning Toby was inside the Michigan state line. Dearborn was only forty minutes away.

Even in the non-sleep state he was in, he couldn't be sure he was actually awake. It was like he was watching himself on the screen, watching a man he didn't know making preparations for mass murder. He turned off Interstate 75 at the thirty five mile marker, found Telegraph Avenue, and drove north for nine miles. At a large shopping area, he pulled in, set his parking brakes, and made his final preparations. He looked at his enlarged maps of the local neighborhood and studied them thoroughly. The mosque he was targeting appeared to be in the middle of a block of small businesses and a few private residences. It was on the east side of a four lane street and the photos indicated its semi-circular entrance driveway was large enough to get an eighteen wheeler in. He wouldn't need to get the trailer out, only the tractor. The facility had ample parking in the rear which could park three hundred cars. Toby was hoping there would not be any vehicles parked in the front entrance driveway. In the event that there were, he felt sure he could get the truck up close enough to the building from one of two other possible approaches.

Next, he removed his three weapons from the bunk area, loaded all three, put the rifle and twelve gauge in the floorboard in front of the passenger seat, and strapped on the .38 automatic in a shoulder harness. He double checked his cell phone, the charge in it, and the phone number on the preset that he had labeled KAMTAP. He got out of the truck and lowered the landing gear to about 3 inches above ground level, and got back in the cab. During his final preparations Toby did not pray.

The Muslim leadership council had convened on time. The five hundred local Muslims whose desire it was to cover the conference with prayer to Allah turned out to be more than eight hundred. The Muslim leaders who would conduct most of their business behind closed doors first addressed the throngs with messages lifting up Allah and the Prophet Mohammed. There were two who felt uncomfortable in such a public setting, especially with a small contingent of press on hand, including one local TV photo journalist, cameraman and all. "Sayyid Qutb, you know how foolish it is for us to be taking chances like this. The Great Satan may have agents infiltrated among our brothers even as we speak," said Mammoud Walid.

"Yes, I suppose it is possible, but we must trust Allah in all things. If we do, our security should be of no concern," Sayyid Qutb retorted.

Both men had been connected to money funneling to Al-Qaeda prior to 9-11 and since. Toby had discovered their identities in his research on the internet. When he discovered they would be in attendance at the conference, that's when this particular mosque on this particular day became his priority target. It was at that time that he had relegated the Syrian and Iranian Embassies in Washington DC to lower priority targets.

Toby pulled out of the shopping area and after two turns and maybe ten city blocks, he found himself northbound on the street the mosque was on. It was 12:26 p.m. and by Toby's estimation, the late stragglers should be in the mosque by now. The conference should be well under way, and hopefully, there would be little or no activity outside. He drove up the street ten mph under the thirty-five mph speed limit. Then, half a block away, he could see the mosque and the semi circular entrance to the building. It was going to be very tight. He swung the seventy-two foot long truck way left, crossing the two southbound lanes, nearly climbing the curb with his left steer tire. Then he started pulling the wheel hard back to the right. It was at this time that he noticed two cars were parked on the left of the entrance drive. He also noticed two large men in dark suits emerge from the front door area. They were violently trying to wave him off. Toby ignored them and brought the nose of his tractor well into the entrance drive. Scanning his right side mirrors, he could see he was already into the tan SUV parked on the right curb. The heavier trailer simply crumpled the front end of the SUV, flattened the right front tire, and pushed it up on the side walk. The two big men were closing fast, coming at Toby from his side, both now leveling their firearms at Toby through the open window, and screaming for him to stop. Toby had the twelve gauge in an instant and unloaded two rounds into each of them, then got back to the steering wheel. The tractor was now past the ninety degree point of the semi circle and again the mirrors, this time on the driver's side, framed the two cars sitting there getting a full broadside crunch from the bomb trailer. Just a bit further and Toby would have the trailer up as close to the front entrance as possible. He reached down to the two steel rods and quickly jammed them to the right. He immediately heard and felt the fifth wheel locking arm release and the apron on the bottom of the trailer slide off the fifth wheel itself. The three service lines to the trailers also released freely when he had jammed the rod. Now the trailer was free standing, no more that twenty-five feet from the front doors to the mosque.

Muslims inside were unaware of the danger until the shotgun blasts interrupted Abdul Rahman in mid sentence, "And brothers, every precaution must be taken from this point forward. The security of our holy mosques must become our highest priority. We must be vigilant at all …" When the four successive and unmistakable reports of gunfire invaded the hall from the outside, there was mass panic. Everyone bolted for the exits, and in the pandemonium, a human wedge blocked escape routes.

Toby pulled the tractor out of the other end of the driveway and continued on north, this time about eight mph faster than the speed limit. Two blocks away he pressed the preset KAMTAP on his cell phone and felt the street under his tractor actually ripple.

Chapter Fifteen

Panic, pandemonium, disorientation, Toby was hurled in a mist. He didn't know where he was. His tractor was twisting and coming apart in piercing pieces. It almost seemed as if the truck itself was attacking him. The heat was intense. He couldn't breathe. There was an acrid smoke all around him. Toby wondered, *did his trailer separate? Or had he hauled it along with him. Had he brought this Hell with him? What had he done?*

Exhausted from the events of the last several days, months of fitful, sporadic and disrupted sleep and not wanting to disturb Sarah, Toby had dropped onto the sofa after getting in very late. It wasn't long before his moaning and howling took on an element of suffering and defeat.

It was Carolyn who heard him first. "Daddy, Daddy, are you all right?" Carolyn had never seen him like this before. He was groaning and almost shouting but the words were illegible. He was wet with perspiration and must have been running a high fever. She spoke to him again, but he didn't seem to know anyone was there. She touched his forehead and immediately ran to awaken her mother.

"Toby, Toby, wake up, wake up! It's all right." Sarah had brought him out many times before. She knew how to do it, but she immediately sensed that this one was the worst yet. "Toby, its okay. Come on now. You need to wake up." She shook him and pleaded with him to come out of it.

Toby had always believed the old tale about not waking up from a nightmare meant certain death. It had to be true. If you couldn't wake up, that meant you'd live with the horror forever. Nobody could do that. So he fought to reach out to Sarah's voice, to get closer. He knew it wouldn't be easy. He'd been here before. He remembered each and every time he could see himself imploring her to wake him. Please, please, hear me. Sarah! Wake me up! He would contort and spasm and shake. He tried to scream, but could not get it out. That was the maddening part, the part that would take him under. He was nearly lost now. Was this his last moment?

She was becoming concerned. "Oh, Lord, help Toby, help me wake him up. Father, please help."

Toby could hear her but could not quite break through the torment or the spasms rolling through him. It was as if something was holding him, pinning him down, forcing him to stay in this place of torment. Toby faintly heard Sarah's voice and yet, not her voice. It was a voice of compassion, forgiveness. Like Sarah's voice and like a rushing wind in a storm, penetrating the screeching and hissing obscenities that were being hurled at him. Amidst the din and cacophony he heard another deeper voice, that of an Appalachian Moses, "Father, God, I feel in my spirit that Toby needs you, now, as he has never needed you. Be with him, comfort him. Let him know the Peace that passes all understanding." The voice faded. It was like Toby was hearing each prayer and seeing both, Jabez and Sarah, but the cloud was still thick with smoke and debris. Then he heard another rasping voice. "Oh, Lord, help me, save me, please." It was his voice.

Just as he had felt a strange peace come over him the moment he shot above Billy Waynick, he felt peace now. It enfolded him and he knew it had all been a nightmare – killing Billy Waynick, the truck bomb, the envisioned reality of Armageddon, all of it, but he still could not wake up, and he knew that he must.

Finally Sarah sent Carolyn for a pitcher of cold water and dumped it over Toby's head. She slapped him hard on both sides of his face several times.

Toby felt a freezing cold numb his body, the heavy burden was crushing the life out of him, and he knew that he must act now – or never. "No! No! No! AHHHHA. No! My God No!" Toby bolted upright. He was home.

In his delirium he had knocked Sarah halfway across the room, but he was awake, finally.

His loving, beautiful, wonderful wife, Sarah, rushed to him and held him, rocked him like a baby and kissed his neck and his face. She soothed him, caressed his head, his hair, his face. She loved him. She consoled him, touched him, held him in her arms and comforted him. He would cry in her arms for nearly an hour. Then he went to the bathroom. Sarah heard the shower come on, and she went to the kitchen to make fresh, hot coffee.

The dream had been two weeks ago, and the dark afterglow of Toby's world-ending, nightmare odyssey still bothered him. For the first few days after the episode, he was afraid to sleep for fear of the same horror returning, or, God forbid, something worse. Gradually, he crawled out of the dark cave he had put himself in. He was still Toby, still the same guy. He was ultra conservative as far as politics and the war on terror were concerned, but his priorities had changed. He had what he'd heard someone call, a paradigm shift. Now, making an honest living for Sarah and the kids, trying to give back even half the love they so easily poured out on him every day had become his new focus.

It might have been expected that his truck driving days would be numbered now that he had abandoned all his murderous plots. It was just the opposite. Toby decided to become a real truck driver. His driving now was to see how good a driver he could become. He realized he took pride in what he was doing. Before, in all the plans and preparations to kill terrorists, he was mostly interested in the truck as being a means to an end. Now he saw himself as a rookie truck driver who wanted to be good at his job. He wanted to learn all he could about trucking and be treated with respect and to treat others in the same manner. Yes, he was climbing out of the hole. Everyday he felt a little stronger, and everyday he prayed for forgiveness and direction.

His plot to kill, to do something in retaliation for 9-11, had died within him, but he still had a little tidying up to do. His barn still hid nearly six tons of ammonia nitrate, twenty barrels of fuel oil, and an electronic detonation device. The day after the nightmare, he had come clean with Sarah. He explained the entire mass murder plot he had devised and nearly acted on. He told her of his amazement that he had dreamed every detail to precision in the horrible nightmare. He told her how real it seemed, including the span of time. It was if he had done everything he had planned, even up to the point where he dropped the bomb trailer twenty-five feet away from the front door of the mosque. He told her how real the screams and panic had sounded.

Toby also had a long talk with Carolyn and convinced her he knew enough about what happened on the golf course that she might as well tell him exactly the real story. "It would clear the air," he said. He convinced her he could deal with whatever actually happened and not go after Billy.

Carolyn realized that he was sincere, so she told him the brief details. "Daddy, he tried to, you know, he tried to rape me. But, Coon Dog was there and stopped him. Billy chased me, knocked me down and hit me. He tore my shirt. Then Coon Dog grabbed him from behind and threw him off me. He really tore into Billy. I was so glad to see him, so glad he helped and so surprised that Billy could have done that. Afterward, I was really crying bad. I mean I was really scared. I got over it. I'm okay. Really, I am. But, Daddy, as scared as I was for me, I was more scared thinking about how you would react if you found out."

Toby took her close to him and gently wrapped her up in his arms. "Are you sure everything is okay now?"

She wasn't crying or shaking or anything like that. She was totally composed, but to Toby she still sounded like a little girl. "Daddy, what makes people want to hurt other people?"

"I don't know honey. I don't know. With Billy, it's a sickness. But, we've all of us got things that will push us over the edge. Sometimes we can hurt people as payback, but I guess, we mostly hurt ourselves when we do that." Toby hadn't said anything to the kids as to the real reason for his nightmare episode. They already thought he was whacked out. Now he just wanted to be a Dad to them. Instead of the ruler of the family, he wanted to be a good example and mentor.

Toby's next trip out would be for eighteen days. The initial run was to Knoxville, Tennessee and back. He could easily have done it in one day, but since he'd asked Derrick to come along with him, he made an overnight trip out of it. Derrick jumped on the chance, especially since it meant two days out of school. They delivered the load by 1:00 p.m., parked the big truck, rented a car and drove up high in the Smokies. Tent pitched and campfire blazing they roasted hot dogs and ate the delicious fruit salad Sarah had packed for them. After marshmallows and coffee, they laid back and looked straight up at the panorama of heaven's twinkling little blue sapphires, scattered above by God's playing with them. Toby enjoyed his time with his son in a new and special way. Their conversation told Toby how much his son had grown and how important this time was.

The next day Toby reluctantly returned Derrick to Lake Thomas and picked up his next load, which was due in El Paso in two days. On his way down he determined that the best way to get rid of the problem back in his barn would be to simply return it to the farmers he had bought it from. He wouldn't ask for a refund. He readily accepted the mistakes he'd made and the financial losses incurred. He relegated both to 'stupid tax' he would gladly pay. He planned to rent a thirty-five foot straight truck, load the barrels of ammonia nitrate fertilizer and fuel oil, then return the fertilizer to the farmers he had purchased it from and give the fuel oil to several families he knew could use it. By using a large straight truck he could do the job easily in only one day as opposed to several days if he returned the stuff in his pick up. He made a mental note to be sure to also take the detonation device away from his barn. He would have no use for it, and he wanted to be done with the whole business.

That night he parked near Dallas. He'd been on the CB with a couple of other drivers who were also headed down towards El Paso. The three of them tried to drink up most of the beer and eat up most of the fajitas in a run down Tex-Mex eatery. When he got back to his truck, he slumped back in the bunk and got the best night's sleep he'd had in years.

Chapter Sixteen

The next morning the three drivers were rolling when the sun burned through the east Texas sky. By noon they were forty miles west of Abilene and were playing trucking games like kids. Steve, an owner operator from Kentucky, was running the front door and said he'd just come up on a bear who was also west bound but was cruising just under the speed limit, "You fellers better slow it down a bit. This ol' full grown bear is trying something." Then Steve stomped on his pedal and quickly got out of CB range. He put twelve miles between himself and the two suckers behind him. When they caught up, Steve had his rig over on the shoulder as they whizzed by.

"Hey, what kind of a front door are you," Toby quipped. "We ain't heard nothing on the CB. Where'd that bear go you warned us about?"

"Bear? What bear?" Steve came back. "I just wanted a little peace and quite so I could enjoy this cup of hot java I just brewed up!"

They raced, lied about the women in their lives, told jokes, and told stories – trucking stories, for the rest of the day. Steve told them about a day a few years back he said he'd never forget. "I was northbound on I-65, forty-five miles from Indianapolis. There was plenty of packed snow and ice on the road. I'd been talking to the driver of a southbound truck who all of a sudden broke off the conversation and yelled through the mike. 'Oh crap! I'm loosing it! I'm coming over! I'm sliding over!'

"At first I wasn't sure what was happening, but it didn't take long to find out. Through the gray, snowy windshield of my truck I could see a big rig in the middle of the median coming my way. I could see that in a matter of seconds that rig would be all the way over into the northbound lanes. I also realized that he had my own truck zeroed in for a head-on collision. Ice be damned, I thought. I yanked that wheel right, trying to keep it under control as I aimed it as far right as possible without actually going in the ditch. About the time I was trying to slow it down on the right shoulder, that out of control southbound truck slid by me, less than six feet away! That other driver, he run through a series of cuss words I've never heard before, and probably will never hear again. It was the closest I'd ever come to a head-on collision. I shook in my boots for a while, I'll tell ya!"

Steve topped that story with another. "Me and my Dad were team driving back around '71–'72. We was coming down a mountain on US 60 in Arizona and lost the brakes – burned them up to be more accurate. I was driving. At the time I was only twenty four years old. I tried everything I could think and everything Dad suggested, but we was riding a runaway truck. Then there was no emergency runaway truck ramps. So all we could do was hang on. We both thought we'd be dead at any moment. You should a heard us. We turned the air blue! The noise and language we used could have been from another planet. Also, I was so scared that I, well, you know, lost control of my bodily functions, shall we say. Anyway, the only thing that saved us was the fact that when the brakes went out, we'd already negotiated the worst of the curves and hairpin turns. When we finally quit rolling on the straight away down below, we was two miles from the bottom of the mountain!"

Later that evening, almost sundown, Steve and the other trucker turned off the interstate at Odessa where they would drop their loads first thing in the morning. Toby continued on, barreling west, sunglasses shielding his eyes, loving the feel of the wheel in his hand, the truck's sure feel as it rammed its way over the black ribbon through the middle of the desert. He hadn't felt this good maybe his entire life. He and the truck were one. Every drop of diesel the four hundred seventy-five horsepower behemoth burned, pumped more life into Toby. He talked to it as if it were an old friend. He was happy.

That night he stopped near Sierra Blanca about eighty miles east of El Paso. He walked out in the desert maybe a half mile, skirting two rattlers on the way. He sat and talked with God a good long while, mostly thanking His Lord for giving him another chance.

When he got back to the tractor he climbed inside and looked around. Toby thought to himself this is my own little private home, right here. It may only be eight by ten by eight feet high, but I've got everything I need. Well, it would be nice if Sarah was here, but that's not going to happen.

He'd gotten more and more into the habit of reading an hour or two every night before he went to sleep. Until now, his reading had been technical and informative, in preparation for his 'mission'. Tonight, in the bunk he was stripped down to his shorts, a stack of pillows back against the wall, and the reading light aimed squarely at the trucker paperback. He was looking forward to catching up on the adventures of the fearless big-wave surfer named Windjammer. *How did he get from Oahu's exotic North Shore to becoming a drifting hitchhiker on the mainland? And what about the truck driver that had a few good hitchhiking tales of his own?. The book has two very unusual and seemingly incompatible characters to be sure. Where is this thing going?* Toby thought it over for a moment. *Well, there's only one way to find out.* He started reading where he had the page thumbed back.

* * *

The next night in the Ramparts Windjammer was back on duty, coolly playing the role of professional Waikiki bartender. A lot of the regulars commented on all the activities of yesterday at Sunset Beach. The local TV station had aired the footage on the news. Bimbette and Bambi seemed to stay closer to Windjammer this evening than normal.

Charley, a local, gay Chinaman, and one of the most regular of the regulars, made a striking origami work of a surfer on a wave. It was placed on the shelf on the back bar in line with all of his other art that had been multiplying there over the years. Charley was very good at the Japanese paper art. In the line up on the shelve were elephants, flamingos, tigers, dancers, rabbits, even grasshoppers and butterflies. Now there was a surfer. "Windjammer may turn out to be Hawaii's newest celebrity," Charley said.

Curly, a retired rodeo rider and another fixture of the inner circle of six or seven regulars was sitting at the bar next to Charley. He'd been nursing his fourth vodka and tonic and was wavering on the edge of having had one too many. "Charley that celebrity status ain't all it's cracked up to be. Anyway, Windjammer ain't the type to want the focus on himself. Are you Jammer?" Realizing Windjammer was busy and didn't hear him, Curly added, "Well, just take my word on it Chinaman. Ol' Jammer don't want no special 'tention just 'cause he rides waves the way I used to ride bulls."

Charley had seen and heard the vodka take control of his friend Curly many times and only countered with, "Sure Curly, what ever you say my good man."

Windjammer had just sent Bambi scooting back across the room, her tray laden down with Margarita's and Mai Tai's. She nearly bumped into Bill Finch as he made his way from the entrance to the far end of the bar. Windjammer saw him coming and started to fill a beer mug with draft for him. Finch waved him off and when he took his seat at the end said, "Just water, I'm on duty."

Windjammer snapped a perfect crisp salute and an equally crisp, "YES SIR."

When he got back with Bill's water, he said, "So, any more record Blue Fins jump into your boat?"

"No. I'm afraid not. How about you? Any more thirty-eight foot wipeouts since yesterday?"

"Everything was blown out today. Maybe tomorrow." The truth was Windjammer was tiring of all the attention placed on him after yesterday morning.

Finch scanned the bar patrons nearby and convinced that there weren't any faces he recognized he beckoned Windjammer a little closer, "I went ahead and did a little more checking on Loeffler. He left the company over a year ago. He is apparently hell bent on maintaining that growing operation on the Windward side. Look Jammer, I shouldn't even be telling you this stuff. It's just that I don't want to see you end up like your friend Ron Willis." Finch noticed the chill and the surprise from Windjammer's eyes. "Yes, I realized two weeks ago you and Willis had a connection. I saw it in your eyes then, just as I do now. I didn't know what the connection was then, but I do now."

Finch paused and with genuine affection said. "I'm sorry Jammer. I'm sorry it happened to Ron."

The upper bunk in the sleeper birth was plenty warm, even in late winter in the mountains in New Mexico. Maybe that was the trouble – why Windjammer couldn't seem to sleep. Maybe it was too warm. This night his projector continued to play out the story of the latter part of his life. Contrary to his avowed 'code of the road' of no memories, the projector methodically continued to run the memories through Windjammers consciousness. Also, a certain suspicion was setting in that somehow this truck driver he got a ride from had some mysterious connection to the flow of memories.

Before he could make another stab at what was triggering it, the projector was rolling again.

It was July in Waikiki; the co-ed season in full bloom. Windjammer had gone out with four new young beauties, only one of which he really had any romantic interest in. Then one afternoon an old girlfriend called him and invited herself over to Windjammer's apartment. Wendy was the perfect blond beach babe. Hair nearly to her waist, a body that men would kill for, and a happy-go-lucky spirit to boot. Add to all of that a very inquisitive mind and a keen interest in philosophy, and you had a gem of a hippie beach girl. Like many young people in the late sixties and the early seventies she equated drugs with the road to enlightenment. She really *believed* that acid opened the door to other realms. Where many in her crowd knew deep down that the drugs were just an exciting escape, Wendy actually studied the possibilities of world change because of acid.

Her split major of psychology and anthropology was aimed at proving it. She wasted no time wrapping her seductive arms around the always willing Windjammer. After their love making, and with the effects of the acid tabs they had taken just getting started good, she announced the real reason for her visit. "I want you to take me to a party tonight. You are off tonight. Right?"

"Sure Wendy, Wendor, Wendoodle…Wendow, nope Wender. Wend, I'll just call you Wend. Sure I'm ooooffffff tonight, but I'm realy ooooooooonnnnnnnnnn." The acid had performed as she had expected, and now she had Windjammer all to herself. But before she would take him again much later in the night, she would show him off at the party.

By the time they arrived at the party it was ten thirty in the evening. They had smoked reefer all afternoon, dropped two more tabs of acid, and picked up George and Ann on the way to the party. That was Windjammer's idea. It was Wendy's idea to give George and Ann both a tab of acid.

The winding road which climbed up the mountains overlooking Honolulu and Waikiki was called Round Top Drive. If it were Malibu in California, all of the homes would have been suspect for a mudslide disaster. Many of them hung precariously over the edge of the mountain, their weight supported by steel or one foot thick hardwood pillars. Hawaii's volcanic subsurface rarely allowed any mudslides similar to those in California.

What a ride up Round Top the foursome was having! Every curve and every overlook to the city below elicited great OOOH'S and AAAH'S and even greater discussions about the cosmic origins of all those twinkling, blinking lights way down below. Ann wanted to stop and sail out over the city and the twinkling lights with the newly discovered set of wings she possessed.

George was a writer, a deep sea fisherman, an actor, a musician, an ex heavy-weight prize fighter, one of

Jammer's fellow bartenders, an ex Navy man, a world traveler, and Jammer's good friend. Ann was a pretty Canadian who financed her world travels by stopping in places like Hawaii, Paris, Acupolco, and Miami where she practiced her cocktail waitress trade. She had a wonderful openness about her. She trusted people, and like most of the rest in Windjammer's circle, she loved drugs and sex.

George and Ann had just returned from Japan. Their plans to travel across Russia on the Trans Siberian Railroad had been abandoned. It seems that George's interest in Sumo Wrestling and Sake somehow drained their meager financial resources. So, here they were back in Hawaii – home base.

Near the top of the mountain Wendy spotted the big luxuriant spread where a very hip affair seemed to be going strong. Windjammer pulled in and as they were exiting his VW surfer van a cloud of sweet Mary Jane perfume swept over them. A band somewhere was playing the Rolling Stone's, Wild Horses. Three large golden retrievers, tails wagging, big friendly doggy smiles, trotted up to greet them. Tiki candles cast multicolored vibrations of lights on the plumeria, hibiscus, choleras, wisteria, banana trees, palm trees, and giant eucalyptus trees waving high above everthing in the perfect ocean breeze floating up the side of the mountain. Couples strolled about. Groups of singles were here and there laughing and sipping cocktails. Lavish tables of hors de oeuvres were scattered about. The cloud of sweet Mary Jane seemed to permeate everything.

George said, "Good people, I think we have arrived."

Wendy spotted her friends who had invited her. She took Ann with her to meet them. Windjammer and George drifted around until they found the bar where they both took a beer. They recognized some people they knew. They did a lot of backslapping and made comparisons of the states of inebriation they were in. They continued to drift and to smoke joint after joint that were being continually passed around. The two tabs of acid, the Mary Jane, and the alcohol were building a train wreck in Jammer. The engine was about to de-rail taking the whole train down the side of this psychedelic mountain in Paradise.

All it took for this to happen was the sight of Richard Loeffler.

There he was! In the center of a throng of admirers – thanking everyone for coming. So, this is *his* pad, *his* dope party. *I wonder how many people died for him to afford a spread like this? How many fat-cat Vietnamese paid him off to get them out. And how many poor boat-people drowned at sea? Ron Willis, Ron old friend, this animal was responsible for your death also!*

Circuits snapped. His brain was fried. He was walking towards the center of the crowd of people. He didn't feel much of anything, not yet. He just waded in through the crowd.

Loeffler saw him coming and caught the thousand yard stare in his eyes. Only this thousand yard stare had a train of acid rolling right through it.

Windjammer was in the field again, in the boonies, humping it. But he had no weapon. His jungle fatigues were shredded and bloody. Most of his squad was two klicks back, being over-run by an NVA company-strength unit in the ville that Windjammer warned his sergeant they should stay out of. After they were pinned down by machine gun and small arms fire, they took direct mortar rounds right on top of them. Jammer and two others were actually blown out of the hole they were in. Those two were goners. They absorbed most of the blast and saved Jammer's life. He ran blind for two minutes, then his vision began to return. He just kept running from the noise. Twenty minutes later he slowed to a trot, then he walked. He and another survivor humped it six more hours until they were air evacuated out.

Now, he was humping again. He stopped two feet in front of Loeffler, but he was seeing his old sergeant. "There it is Sergeant. I told you. There it is. Didn't I tell you? Look what we got now. We got nothing. There it is man. We got nothing."

Another circuit overloaded, maybe ten, and the acid train jumped the rails. Windjammer went for Loeffler's throat and tried a groin kick. Loeffler was no patsy. He sidestepped the groin kick and got in close to Windjammer with an Aikido move and nearly brought him down. In doing so he gave Windjammer a one time shot at his right ear, and Windjammer took it in his teeth and shook it like a pit bull. It lasted another six seconds, and Windjammer spit the ear out. Now that his head was free again Loeffler used it to sledgehammer the surfer square on his nose, breaking it. This blew a couple more circuit breakers in Winjammer's torched and scorched brain. He bear-hugged Loeffler and drug him through a sliding door window to the railing on a balcony overlooking the city below. He had him halfway up the railing and was going to throw him over. George got there just in time and with the help of two other men he was able to get between Jammer and Loeffler.

Driving down the mountain, George had his hands full. Jammer wanted to go back. Ann wanted to leap out the window into flight, and Wendy after her third tab of acid, kept proclaiming that world peace and world-wide nirvana were here at last.

* * *

It was very late. Toby set the book aside, and fell off to sleep.

Toby was hoping he'd run into Jabez sometime in the next fourteen days. He wanted to tell Jabez about this new direction his life seemed to be taking. His route took him from El Paso, where Toby delivered a load, to a large retail distribution center in Kansas City. Next, he ran regional loads for the next three days. Then, he was dispatched through the upper Midwest. He then went to Iowa, Minnesota, Wisconsin, and Illinois. A couple of nights later, in a truck stop outside the tiny farm town of Ladysmith, Wisconsin, Toby fueled his truck and was walking in to sign the fuel ticket. He noticed a black woman sitting on a bench just outside the entrance and at first didn't notice anything unusual, but as he walked past her he could see she brought her gaze up and was looking directly into his face. It wasn't that she was initiating intense eye contact; it was more like a plea that she be recognized.

Toby walked on inside and told himself she was probably a panhandler, and he would maybe give her some change on his way out. After he completed his business inside, he walked back out. The black lady was still there, and again she gazed up into his face. Toby decided to sit next to her and see if he could figure out her story.

"How ya' doing?" Toby asked the woman. She was clean, had on white pants and a red top. She had on some red lipstick, and her hair was short and in place. Early fifties would have been close to her age, and although she appeared to be clean and well kept, Toby noticed her hands and nails were rough.

"I'm tryin' to get some money fo' some food, just a sandwich or somethin'. I ain't had nuthin' since yesta'day."

Toby gave her six dollars and asked her, "Where you from?"

"Nawlins'."

Toby understood her to be saying New Orleans. "What are you doing way up here?"

"I had to leave. Just been getting' a bad feelin' bout' stayin' in Nawlins'."

"What do you mean?"

"Don't rightly know, only that I felt I had to get away from down there."

A black truck driver walked by and handed the woman some money. He and the woman laughed at something. Toby didn't catch it.

"Ya' know, some a' these men, not him, others, walk by me and want to know if I'll do some things for em'. Ya' know, nasty things. It hurts me for them to talk like that to me."

Understanding the implication, Toby said, "Yes, I know what you mean."

They were both quiet for a moment, then Toby got up and said, "Well, I'd better get on down the road. Good luck to you."

"God bless you, Toby."

He stopped and looked back, "How did you know …?"

She cut him off, "Jabez told me about you, honey chile', and he said to tell you he'll be seeing you soon."

Toby walked away chuckling to himself.   He was not surprised.

* * *

That night he was rolling southwest directly into the teeth of a vicious late spring thunder storm. The black and gray clouds when silhouetted by the brilliant fluorescent lightning flashes made the earth look as though berserk giants were roaming around inside a huge cavern. He thought back to the chance encounter with the woman at the truck stop. There was nothing more she had for him, only that Jabez would see him soon.

The storm intensified. His truck wavered all over the highway, but he was intent on riding it out. Many were the nights he had slowed more than the others or on occasion pulled off the road to let a particularly violent storm pass by. He admired the drivers who rolled on through the bad ones. Visibility nearly non-existent, raining so hard the roof of the cab sounded like escaping prisoners pounding it with sledge hammers, the road slippery, 'greasy' as many truckers described it. They still rolled on. Tonight Toby would roll on, getting happier and more confident with each howling wind gust and fearsome bolt of lightning.

The next few days Toby kept an attentive ear on the CB. Now, he felt sure he would be crossing paths with Jabez again. He also found himself making plans to visit some old friends that had scattered across the country. He thought that driving a big truck afforded the perfect opportunity to do so. His mind wandered back over the years. What were these old friends doing? How had their lives worked out? Most of them he hadn't seen in twenty-five years. He replayed the old memories, some good and some not so good. The endless hours behind the wheel allowed him ample opportunity to replay old relationships. He reflected on what might have happened if things had gone just slightly differently than they had. What if a good buddy hadn't married so and so? What if that family from the north hadn't moved into Forest Park, Georgia, a town his family had lived in when he was young? Would he ever have learned anything about the rest of the world? What if, what if? He played out scenario after scenario, and finally he concluded he probably wouldn't change a thing if he'd been given the opportunity, that is, except his crazy bomb plot. He loved Sarah and the kids deeply. He loved his farm. He loved the South, and he loved the United

States. He was beginning to love this crazy business of pulling eighty thousand pounds down the road. After he tired of reshaping the past, he would think about this new love. How long would he continue driving? He thought about a verse in the song he'd heard Jabez sing…

> **"Now I started truck driving to see if I could,**
> **Now I'm driving forever, I knew that I would"**

Then he thought about another verse…

> **"Yes, I'll die on your highway, and if they will fit,**
> **My brakes and my drive shaft right there they will sit"**

Would he die on the highway? His mind wandered. The miles in front of him rolled on, winding along. He was alone out there on this black ribbon that never stopped. Perhaps the real question was not would he die, but rather, how would he live?

Toby only had a couple of days left on this trip before he'd be turning for home. He still hadn't heard from or seen Jabez, but one night in Oklahoma he caught the tail-end of a song another driver was singing. *Boy! That sounded like something Jabez would sing.* Toby keyed his mike, "Breaker one-nine. Hey driver, that song you just sung , I missed most of it. Would you sing it again?"

"Well, I'll give her another try at it. I just heard it myself the other day."

Toby came back. "Where did you hear it from?"

The driver said, "An old preacher man up in Michigan was singing it the other day. He said he'd been singing it for a long time but didn't remember where it came from." Then he started in:

"It was late one night in the blinding snow
I was about thirty miles out of Kokomo
I left the highway doing ninety-eight
There ain't no doubt, I was feelin' great.

Well things started goin' bad real quick
Sure the old highway was icy and slick
But I reckon what killed me, I'm sure you'd know
Was the hole in my heart, and the loss of my soul.

The drugs and the booze had kind of pushed things
along
And I remembered writin' all those crazy songs
But the real problem is, I think you'll see
Is what lies before me in eternity.

Now the time is here and it can not wait
But OOOH, my highway don't lead to the pearly gate
No, I'm a goin' to hell, and I'm a goin' there quick
This damned old truck has done the trick.

And I reckon what I'll find down there below
Is a bunch of truck drivers with an empty load
So listen to me brothers, it'll save some time
If you don't want to go to hell, you gotta' drive
that line.

And be real careful in the blinding snow
When you're about thirty miles outta Kokomo
And don't leave the highway doing ninety-eight
Cause if you don't know Jesus, it'll be too late."

A big smile lit up Toby's face. That song had Jabez written all over it. It had to be from Jabez. Maybe that's what the black woman meant, "He'll be seeing you soon." He felt like anything was possible with Jabez. Surprisingly, Jabez never showed up on this eighteen day trip. The next day Toby picked up a load in New Mexico and turned away from the setting sun. He was going east, towards Alabama, towards home.

Sarah was always glad to see Toby when he'd get back home from a long trip. It was a little strange to get in bed with a man after nearly three weeks of sleeping alone, but after those first few unsure minutes, the old familiar feelings re-emerged and soon they would be carried along a path of love making not unlike their first few times together twenty-five years earlier.

Toby came in the house by the back door. It was Saturday morning. Toby knew she was probably puttering around in the kitchen. He hadn't seen her in the yard where she would be found on many a spring Saturday morning.

"Hey there stranger, I heard the truck when you pulled in." Sarah came to him, and he opened his big arms and brought her close to him. He loved the feel of her and the smell of spring in her hair and on her skin.

"I missed you so much," he said.

"Me too," she purred.

She made him breakfast and brought him up to date on everything, and then said, "It's probably silly, but I've seen a car over across the road twice. I just thought it strange. I didn't even see who was in it, but I, well I just thought it was weird. I'm sure it's nothing. I shouldn't have mentioned it."

"A car? What kind of a car?" Toby was spreading butter on his biscuit.

"It was dark, maybe black. It didn't stay long, either time." She was putting the milk back in the fridge.

"Well, maybe it'll come back while I'm home. I'll go out and see who it is. You know the Burkes are selling. Maybe a would-be buyer was scouting the neighborhood."

"Yeah, I'll bet that's it. So what's on your agenda the next three days?"

"Oh nothing exciting, other than trying to seduce a beautiful woman I know," then he added, "I *do* have a chore that must be done out by the barn."

"What's that?"

"The stuff I would have made the bomb with, I need to get it out of the barn. I'm going to take it back to the farmers I got it from."

"The sooner the better, right?" Sarah said.

"Right," Toby said.

Sarah was finished in the kitchen and started for the bathroom and a hot shower where she knew Toby would follow her.

Monday morning Toby was up at the crack of dawn. He was in the kitchen having coffee and planning the day ahead, his last day at home. He wanted to get the ammonia nitrate and fuel oil cleared out of the barn and taken back to the farmers and the two families he had selected for the fuel oil. He wanted to be done with it all by noon. Then he planned on a quick trip to Coon Dog's. The 30/30 deer rifle and the .38 automatic would otherwise have ended up in a dumpster.

After that, he was going to meet Derrick and Carolyn at the golf course and play nine holes, eighteen if they could squeeze it in. Then he, Derrick, and Carolyn were meeting Sarah at the best restaurant in town. They all marveled at Toby's new-found zest for life. He'd never exactly been a stick in the mud, but he'd also never exhibited the enthusiasm to do things with his family that he was so obviously caught up in now.

Toby had picked up the rental truck Saturday afternoon, and this morning it was backed up to the open barn doors, its roll-up door all the way up. Toby used a wooden ramp to roll the barrels onto the truck with a heavy duty two-wheel dolly. Then he used his new four foot long steel wrecking bar to help position the barrels once they were on board.

Across the road from Toby's farm there was a black SUV hidden a hundred yards deep in the trees that started a quarter of a mile from the road. The early morning dew was thick on it, but the vehicle had no occupants inside. They were closer to the tree line and were completely undetectable in their camouflage BDU's.

FBI special agent Dean Hollister had his field glasses trained on the activity at Toby's barn, "Looks like he's got most of it on board." He could see just enough through the space between the truck and the barn to get a pretty good idea of what was going on.

"Roger that," special agent in charge Brandon Sullivan said from his command post inside what appeared to be an old two-ton panel truck, some six miles away.

"He's rolling the door down," Hollister said into his mike.

"Copy that Dean," said Sullivan.

Toby was wet from the labor. He dried off with a towel and changed to a dry shirt. He retrieved the 30/30 deer rifle and the .38 automatic from a cabinet he'd been keeping them in, and on the way to the truck he picked up the wrecking bar he forgot to put in with the load before he closed the roll-down door. He walked out of the barn, opened the door to the cab on the passenger side, placed all three inside, and closed the door.

"He just put his weapons up front in the cab. Looked like a hunting rifle, a handgun, and maybe a shotgun. There were three."

"Copy that Dean. Three weapons on board in the cab. What's he doing now?"

The other special agent assigned to the stake out with Hollister was Wayne Spinoza. He answered up this time, "Suspect has gone back in the barn. I can't see what he's doing." Spinoza adjusted the microphone near his lips. "You copy that agent Sullivan?"

"Ten-four. Copy he's back in the barn," Sullivan replied. Then he took the opportunity to remind the entire team, "Gentlemen, do not forget, when he starts, *if* he starts rolling, you must be prepared to take him out if he shows anything suspicious at all. I don't have to remind you that we would like to see if this is a hand off to another suspect. If he is indeed in route to a target, well that's a call I'll make as this thing progresses. Remember, we've let him go this far simply because we have felt he might lead us to other players. But, the bottom line is this, take him out if you have any questions about what he's doing."

Sullivan then heard the same identical message back to him from Hollister, Spinoza, and the three other mobile units in the area; "Ten-four on that agent Sullivan. Copy that."

Finally Toby emerged from the barn with the detonator. The wiring to the fuse was easy to disassemble, as were the other components, but looking through field glasses over a quarter mile away, it was impossible to see that the detonator had been destroyed.

Spinoza reported in to special agent in charge Sullivan, "Suspect coming out of the barn. He's got the detonator. He's putting the detonator in the cab."

"Copy that Wayne," Sullivan responded. "He must be planning on making a stop on the way to the target to open the back door and install the detonator. Probably doesn't want to risk a premature detonation while in transit."

This time it was Hollister, "Roger that. Suspect appears to be done here. He's getting behind the wheel. Now he's rolling away from the barn. Okay, suspect on the highway rolling northbound."

"Copy that Dean. Continue mobile surveillance from his rear. Team Two, he's rolling your way. ETA to your position is two minutes. All right gentlemen, let's don't lose this bird."

Toby was anxious to get to the first farm on his list and start unloading. He had driven only two miles when he thought he felt a barrel come loose in the back. He pulled over on the shoulder. He would grab the wrecking bar and go back to readjust the loose barrel and this time strap it down even tighter.

Team Two special agent Eddie McPherson was very alarmed, "Command, we got a problem. I think he spotted us when he went by. He's pulled over to the shoulder."

"Ten-four Eddie, don't leave your position. Let's just see what he's doing," were the instructions from Sullivan.

McPherson's partner on Team Two was special agent Geoffrey Dean, and he already had his Type .308 McMillan bolt action sniper rifle zeroed in on Toby's head through the driver's side window. He could still hear Sullivan's recent instructions ringing in his ears, "Bottom line, take him out if you have any questions."

Toby opened his door, then reached over to grab the wrecking bar, it's shiny new black paint glistening in the early morning sunlight like the barrel of a well oiled and well maintained shotgun.

When Toby stepped out, Special agent McPherson said, "Easy now, Geof; let's just see what he's up to."

But Geoffrey Dean caught the glint of sunlight on the wrecking bar and said, "He's got the shotgun," and again Sullivan's words rang in his ears, "Take him out if you have any questions."

When Toby turned to close the door, special agent Dean put the cross hairs of the Leopold Mach 4 tactical scope between Toby's eyes. Special agent Dean took a deep breathe and prepared to squeeze the trigger.

Chapter Seventeen

Jabez had one of his premonitions in up-state New York. He knew he had to get down to Alabama to help Toby. He turned around on a dime and drove all night straight through to Lake Thomas, Alabama. Now it was morning, and Jabez knew time was running out. He had to find Toby! He drove through the small town twice with no luck. He decided to check the secondary feeder roads into town. There! There up ahead!

There he was, pulled over on the shoulder standing outside the cab of a straight truck with a wrecking bar in his hand. *What's that up ahead a hundred and thirty yards? Oh no! Someone is drawing a bead on Toby with a rifle!*

Jabez jumped on his brakes and swung his big truck across the median nearly tipping his trailer. The air brakes coughing and the air horn screaming, the big truck slid to a stop on the shoulder in a cloud of dust. He had Toby and the straight truck blocked from the shooter.

"What the … ?!" McPherson and Dean blurted out simultaneously. McPherson was on the horn to Sullivan. "Agent Sullivan we got a semi that pulled up in front of the suspect. He's got the straight truck totally blocked from our view."

Special agent in charge Brandon Sullivan said, "Crap! Okay we're going to have to close down on him. All teams converge on team two's position, and step on it! Activate all your lights and sirens. I want a perimeter around those two trucks."

Jabez was climbing down out of his cab and saw Toby walking towards him. Immediately they saw and heard flashing lights and sirens converge on them from all directions. Team two, agents McPherson and Dean, waited for agent-in-charge Sullivan. By the time he arrived they were already able to confirm that the suspected shotgun was actually a wrecking bar and the detonator had been destroyed. Sullivan asked McPherson, "What about the rifle and handgun?"

"They were still in the cab, unloaded."

Sullivan did a thorough inspection of both vehicles and had a background check, MVR, and registration check run on Jabez, his tractor, and his trailer. He was in no hurry, everything thorough and by the book. Finally he approached the two men in handcuffs and said, "I sure hope you two have a good story to tell."

An hour later Sullivan was completing his written report of the surveillance of Toby Etheridge, including the tailing of the straight truck and the not quite plausible arrival of a semi-tractor trailer. There was nothing stated about an innocent man nearly having been assassinated by the FBI.

That night Toby and Jabez were at the edge of the woods near his house. They were enjoying a hickory campfire and uncountable galaxies of stars twinkling above. Earlier they had polished off country ham, fried chicken, mashed potatoes and gravy, green beans, turnip greens, corn bread, and blackberry cobbler. Sarah had gone all out when Toby informed her that Jabez would be staying over the night.

"You know, there's a lot of things I'd like to ask you. But it's kinda' like I don't really need to. I mean, there's a lot I don't understand. At the same time, I have this feeling that maybe, maybe I don't have to understand it all, particularly your role in all that has gone on. Am I making any sense?"

They were leaning back in huge wooden chairs with great big wooden arm rests and a neck brace so you could gaze comfortably at the galaxies above. Jabez started, "I don't rightly know if I could answer any of your questions, but here's something to think about. The focus should not be on me. Look, you believe that God shows you signs. Right? Certain significant, let's say quirks of reality. Right? You believe that don't you?"

Toby was thinking, *there he goes again, reading my mind.* "Yes, I believe that."

"You and I aren't any different, you know. I believe the same thing. I believe The Father shows me signs as well. You want to ask how these quirks of reality are put in motion. You want to know why and how The Father has brought us together. You want to know everything abut how it all works. Right?"

Toby nodded.

"We all want to know these things. But none of that is important to The Father. He just wants us to serve Him and to accept the Lamb's sacrifice on the cross. The focus Toby. Where should your focus be? Yourself? Me? No. Really, Toby, where should it be?"

"On serving The Father and accepting the Lamb's sacrifice."

Chapter Eighteen

The next morning Toby was ready to roll at the crack of dawn. A quick scan out the kitchen window revealed an empty pad near the barn. Jabez was gone, probably on his way back to New York. Toby couldn't help but wonder if Jabez was on the CB holding a sunrise session of his "truck driver's ministry."

Before he climbed in his truck, he fell to his knees and prayed more intensely than he had in the past. Petitions were made that he would redirect his life more to serving The Father and to witnessing for Jesus. That night he was in Oklahoma, and the day had gone very well. Did he not notice just a little something different all day? Something stirring in Him? Somehow many more CB contacts he had made today seemed to be with drivers like him – centered on God. His prayers tonight were similar to his morning prayers. He also prayed for the United States of America, its leaders, and all of its fighting men. No, Toby would probably never be able to pay the price that many in his Vietnam generation had paid, but he felt that from now on he could at least support with prayer those caught up in the fray of the current war. How was this current war on terror going to play out? Toby knew that his role from here on out was to be a prayer warrior. He thought about what that meant. The commitment required in order to be serious about it. All he knew was that it was time. Time to come to God once again, with yet another commitment to be better this time, to be closer, to try harder. But he was tired tonight. It had been a long day behind the wheel. He wanted to put off any more of the new commitment, simply trying harder and identifying his role as a prayer warrior. He wanted to relax a little before he went to sleep.

He leaned back in the sleeper and picked up the trucker paperback. He seemed to recall that Windjammer's friend George had just barely prevented Windjammer from throwing Richard Loeffler over the railing to the city of Honolulu below. *Where was it? Oh yeah, there it is.* He reread the sentence where George had driven all four party goers down acid mountain and started reading fresh again from that point.

* * *

It was about a month after the near disastrous party night up Round Top Drive on top acid mountain. George Russo, Windjammer, Sven Torger, and Jerry Carmody were hiking in Palolo Valley. Sven had promised them all there was ample reward awaiting them at the end of the trail. Sven had some plants growing up there, and of course there was the Palolo Valley water falls and the pool below they could swim in. Tropical ferns of every size, shade, and shape seemed to be everywhere. The lush vegetation in this Oahu valley so very close to Waikiki and Diamond Head could simply overwhelm anyone. There were the native Hapu, Ama'u, and Ulule ferns. There were native Hibiscus, Koa trees, and Sandalwood trees (Iliaki). There were plants and trees introduced by ancient Polynesians: Bamboo,

Breadfruit, Hukui, and Ginger. Sven knew many of them and was pleased to share his knowledge. Often he would point out plants that were introduced to the islands in the last couple of hundred years: Algaroba, Banyan trees, Taro vines. Mangrove, Lychee, and Bird of Paradise. And of course the plant he was the most familiar with, Cannabis Sativa.

This foursome felt very much at home in the beauty of this valley. They could be found hiking its very narrow trail on a regular basis. The trail hugged the side of Wa'Ahila ridge and if followed all the way to the top, you would be nearly two thousand feet above sea level and have incredible views of both sides of the island.

"Carmody, quit dragging your ass," quipped Sven as they negotiated yet another tiny passageway on the trail. Vegetation covered mountain would be all over your left shoulder, drop off to the creek eighty feet below to your right, and an eight inch wide trail under foot.

"Why do I always drag this crew of rejects and misfits up this mountain? Why?" Sven added loudly from his position at the front of the line.

"Because you love us so," Carmody shouted twenty yards behind Sven. Windjammer and George took the two and three positions on the very narrow mountain trail. George was ready for another toke on the weed being passed up and down the line.

"Jammer, are you Bogarting that joint again?"

"Bogarting? I don't think so, but I *am* ready to eat it. Okay, here, as if your wildly roaming, wildly, hallucinogenic, wildly fanciful imagination needed any more fuel." He passed the joint back to George. A look of deep understanding, deep friendship crossed each other's face.

A moment later Carmody piped up, "Where's the weed? How come I'm sucking hind tit back here?"

George choked down a deep drag and passed the reefer back to Carmody, "Well now my good friend, it seems that Jammer insists that this splendid herb is not necessary to enhance, let us say, my more creative side. As for you my dear Mr. Carmody, I believe that the more herb for you the better. You see Mr. Carmody, when an individual such as yourself, let us say when a writer such as yourself reaches that oh so painful career plateau, that plateau we all dread reaching, then my good friend, it is my view that the more inhaled fragrance of the wicked weed, the better."

"I see, I see. Now exactly what career plateau are you referring to? And by the way, knock off this line of bull and pass that joint back here." The two of them exchanged the same deep understanding vibration of friendship that George and Windjammer had exchanged.

When the three hippy writers and one big wave surfer reached Sven's patch of marijuana, they were already lit up quite nicely. Sven said, "Okay fellers take these scissors and clip you off just about a half dozen of the juiciest flower tops you see, and then grab you a dozen or so of the best leaves you see." Everyone did as they were instructed. Then Sven said, "Bring me your harvest fellers, and in a few minutes we'll have us the best, the freshest homegrown that any man has ever impaled – oops – inhaled deep down into those tiny alveoli,...alveolar,...uh... alveenersnitzels,... aw hell, in your lungs." He uncovered a small aluminum outdoor oven – a little hobo oven – and lit a small fire under it. He opened the front door and then placed the four miniature hemp harvest treasures inside and closed the door.

As they waited for the weed to dry, Sven produced a pint of Jim Beam. It passed from hand to hand. Carmody, Windjammer, and George chased the bourbon with water. Sven never chased or mixed anything in his whiskey, that is unless beer happened to be available.

The day wore on. The Palolo Valley homegrown was inhaled. They swam naked in the pool at the base of the water fall. Then they finished the Jim Beam and reluctantly started back down the trail towards the city. What a day it had been! But there would be many more days like it. After all, this was paradise, they were young, and most importantly, like most in their generation believed, they were in control of their destiny.

Windjammer's destiny was about to be altered dramatically and irrefutably beyond his control. His shift at the Ramparts started at 6 p.m. He would lay low and not make much eye contact with anyone for a couple of hours. By then he would probably have unloaded most of the load he was carrying when he and his writer pals came out of the jungle's marijuana haze around 4 p.m. There were nights at the Ramparts that he floated through on one high or another, but he wasn't all that happy with the result of those evenings. Even hard core pot-heads like Windjammer knew they had certain limits they best not exceed.

Many of the lunch hour businessmen who'd stretched their two martini lunch into an all afternoon drink-a–thon greeted Windjammer when he relieved Belle the day shift bartendress. "Hey Windjammer, I'd like to borrow about half of your harem for the evening."

"Yeah, Jammer, me too. But I'll settle for just one cute red-head."

Their attention was diverted when Bimbette and Bambi came on their shift. Now all the sexual innuendo was aimed at them.

Windjammer was pleased that the focus had been shifted away from himself.

Bimbette took one look at him and said privately to him, "Wow. Your eyes look like pan cakes floating through hell."

"Yeah, I know, but I'm cool. In a couple of hours they will be back to normal."

So they were and also in a couple of hours he would be down, off his daytime high, and looking forward to the joints he'd smoke with the bar crew when the Ramparts closed and the doors were locked.

Somewhere around 10 p.m. Windjammer noticed Bill Finch near the entrance to the Ramparts, but instead of coming on in, he beckoned Windjammer to him and signaled he'd wait outside. After a few minutes Windjammer had Bimbette fill in for him, and he walked outside to meet Finch.

"Let's walk around the block." Finch had one of his worried looks.

"Jammer, I've got bad news."

Windjammer lit a cigarette and braced himself for whatever was to follow.

"I'll start at the beginning. Your run-in with Loeffler up on Round Top, well, let's just say that the word got out on that to all the wrong places. The downtown China mafia, somehow it got back to them. Here's the deal. You know good and well they've been wanting to do away with Loeffler. He's really been creating havoc on the windward side, and now we are hearing he's into another operation on the Makaha side. They aren't stupid. They can't afford a regular hit to take him out. The police, the drug task force, everybody will know who did it."

Windjammer had a sickening thought and an equally nauseous trembling hit his stomach. Then Finch confirmed Windjammer's darkest suspicion.

"I can't tell you how I know this, but trust me. They are going to set you up. You have the motive. At least thirty people at Loeffler's party that night would make that testimony. They saw what you did."

They rounded a corner and walked down a sidewalk between two hotels until the sidewalk played out at the beach, at the ocean. Diamond Head jutted out majestically to their left, and couples were walking barefooted in the sand and the moonlight. Palm trees gently swaying, it was the perfect romantic idyllic version of paradise, laid out in front of them. It would be the last night Windjammer would see it, maybe forever. He pondered the possibilities. He didn't have a clue as to what he could do. He did know he didn't want to be anywhere close to the Pake's – the Chinese gangsters downtown that controlled most of the hard core drug traffic, prostitution, vice, extortion, and gambling on Oahu. Their reputation and history of murder and violence was one that even the New York City mafia families would have had difficulty in surpassing.

Finch aimed at a bench by the sea. They both sat down. "Now here's the scary part. We aren't talking a matter of time here. What they are planning is going to happen quickly, maybe tonight. Either they are going to grab you and get your prints all over a piece and leave it at the site they do Loeffler, or it's going to be a double death scenario. You show up to do Loeffler, there's a shootout, and you both buy the farm. You hearing me?"

"I'm afraid so."

"Let me bum a smoke."

Windjammer produced a cigarette and lit Finch up. "Bill, you know I trust you. I've made a mess of a lot of things. I don't know what to do"

The gentle Waikiki trade winds were blowing their hair a little and ruffling their shirts a little." I thought you might say that. Do you want my advice?"

"You know it man."

"Okay, Jammer. You don't have a choice. You gotta blow this island tonight. You know these scum we're talking about. They won't hesitate a second to pull this off. They might be watching us right now. That's why I pulled you out of the Ramparts. You can't wait. Don't let them make the first move Jammer. Believe me, you don't want that to happen."

"Yeah, but look. I can't just disappear. I mean, I don't even..."

Finch jumped in, "I can help you out. You know I can pull a couple of strings here and there. And listen, Jammer, I'm dead serious! They may be watching us now. From the information I have, I guarantee you this won't drag out for another two or three days.

* * *

Windjammer was in Fargo North Dakota. Maybe not as far away from Waikiki as was possible if you only considered mileage. Culturally it could have been a different universe. No Hollywood types here and no big wave surfers. Finch had warned him two weeks ago not to go back home to St. Louis. That was the night Finch dragged him out of the Ramparts and hustled him secretly onto a Navy flight to Moffett Field just north of San Jose. Finch had said don't underestimate the Chinese mafia. They might be waiting for you back in St. Louis.

Windjammer had heeded all of Bill Finch's instructions, even his order that night not to go back to the Ramparts or his apartment. Finch had already gone to Jammer's apartment and collected a few clothes and personal items. Then he personally placed him in a Navy transport plane. The pilot was well versed in the procedures for handling certain types of 'special cargo'. Those situations occurred every now and then.

The next day at 10 a.m. Windjammer was driven off the Moffett Field air station in an unmarked government vehicle and deposited at the Sunnyvale, California, Greyhound Bus Station. Windjammer looked in the envelop Finch had given him and counted out three hundred dollars in twenties. So *this is my new existence. Hustled out of paradise and deposited in California with three hundred bucks to my name. I may not be able to access my own checking account. Finch warned me about trying that.* True to his old existence and his natural spirit he said to himself, *So be it, I'll play it out for awhile and stay cool. Nothing would prevent me from checking with Finch in four or five months and see what, if anything, happens to Loeffler. Hopefully I can go back.*

But what to do in the meantime? Again he was true to his spirit. She was sitting on a bench just outside the Greyhound Station. She appeared to be waiting for someone. She wore faded bell bottom jeans, sandals, a long sleeved tie-dyed top, and matching not cheap strands of beads and puka shells around her neck. She was a real beauty.

He sat next to her and turned his best smile on her, "Where you going?"

"Berkeley. How about you?"

"Yeah, I'm thinking about going to Berkeley too. The problem is I've never been there. You think you could show me around a little?"

"Well, maybe. I have friends coming for me any minute now. If they have room, I'm sure you can ride with us. Where are you from?"

"Hawaii."

"Really? I've always wanted to go. Maybe you could tell me a little about it? I'm April."

Three days later April and Windjammer were strolling through the U.C. Berkeley campus grooving on the pot and cocaine they'd been doing. It looked like a busy place for sure Windjammer thought. Signs were everywhere announcing this protest or that protest. Serious looking activists were scurrying about, most bearded and many wearing worn army jackets. *So this is it* he thought – the center of the opposition to what I was doing in Vietnam. Now that the war was over, there was still plenty for these serious looking people to be squawking about. Watergate, women's lib, and now- days, the environment was becoming their pet protest. *Oh, hell, they just need to smoke a little more pot and drop a little more acid like most of them did a few years back in Haight Ashbury,* he thought.

April took him into the student union dining area, and Windjammer realized he was feeling a little out of place. Many of the serious scurrying activist threw doubtful glances his way. Glances that said, "Surfer beach guy, this isn't your scene. What are you doing here looking like the ocean itself with your bleached out surfer's mop and flowery aloha shirt. What are *you* protesting? What are *you* threatening to blow up? What part of this society are *you* going to burn?"

He wanted to shout out, "I'm just running, that's all," but instead he sat at a table and waited for April to return with sandwiches.

He glanced at a San Francisco newspaper on the table, picked it up and was thumbing through the first several pages when a small headline jumped out at him. *Oahu Police Search For Suspect* It had a Honolulu dateline and was a UPI story. Windjammer looked up to see where April was. She was still in the sandwich line. He read quickly:

Honolulu Police Department spokesman Jeffrey Kaaihue said today that a major search is in progress for what he described as the "primary suspect" in the murder case of Richard Loeffler. Loeffler, a suspected drug king-pin, was gunned down near his showy Round Top Drive residence two days ago. Kaaihue said Loeffler's body was found below an overlook in thick mountainside undergrowth. Police believe the preliminary investigation points to a Waikiki bartender that witnesses said tried to kill Loeffler approximately a month ago.

Kaaihue went on to say that police have reason to believe the suspect has fled the Hawaiian Islands for California. Police would not reveal the suspects name until additional information is compiled. He did note that authorities in California have been requested to provide assistance in the case.

When April returned Windjammer had vanished, and there was no newspaper on the table.

FARGO, NORTH DAKOTA

The snow had started yesterday about noon and had dropped a good eight inches. Today the gray bitter-cold clouds were threatening to open up again on Windjammer's little cabin and swallow it up in a blizzard which the weatherman was calling for. *It's time to head south. Bill and Martha will find someone soon enough. Anyway, I know I was not the best dishwasher they ever had. Early December. I'll be down on the Gulf Coast in a week or less if I have good luck getting rides. Fargo has been good to me. Renting this little cabin has worked out, and I've had plenty of money from the restaurant to buy a lid every two or three weeks. Yep, I have to stretch it out, compared to what I was used to, but maybe that's not such a bad thing anyway. Jill brings enough cocaine to sink a battleship. It'll be a little tough leaving her behind. She's a homebody. I'm sure she won't go on the road with me.*

He got up and walked to the mirror in the bathroom and searched it for the face he remembered, the deep bronzed tan, the sun bleached nearly shoulder length hair, the chiseled jaw line, the winning smile. It was all gone. Now the red-brown beard covered most of it, and the long sun bleached surfer's locks had been replaced by sandy brown, ear-length hair. *They won't ever find me. The old Windjammer has disappeared.*

This guy in the mirror doesn't have any resemblance to him. Except for the eyes. They were the same. They possessed the same spiritual passion they always had, the same okay-what's next, vibrant anticipation they always had. No, they're not going to find me, and he walked away from the mirror and started packing a small travel bag.

Chapter Nineteen

It was dawn in the New Mexico mountains. The truck driver had been up a half hour. He'd been outside seemingly drawing strength from gazing off to the east in anticipation of the coming light. *It's time to tell him. He's never heard the truth other than the CB fallen angel's introduction to it. Well, he's going to hear it this morning, and he will need to make a choice.*

The truck driver went back to his tractor and brewed a pot of coffee. He turned the key and brought the truck to life. The truck shook when the starter hit, then it settled into a noisy dat, dat, dat, dat, dat, dat, idle. The sun was just behind a mountain ridge, and the explosion of color in the sky above was startling. It looked like a strawberry had been attacked by a blow torch.

When the truck started, Windjammer had to shake his head and exert an effort to remember where he was. He nearly fell out of the top bunk when he rolled to stretch. He had only dropped off to sleep two hours ago. The earlier hours of last night had ushered him through the last twenty five years. The memories that his code of the road expressly forbade had held him hostage most of the night.

But last night's memory parade had a different feel to it, as if the entire twenty-five years of running was leading to some plateau, some critical junction. For some strange reason, Windjammer sensed that he was approaching that junction this very day.

"Mornin'. How about a cup of coffee?" The truck driver was in the driver's seat.

"Yes sir. Maybe I will."

The driver had a cup waiting for Windjammer by the time he had climbed down out of the top bunk and made his way into the passenger seat. Windjammer blew over the lip of the cup to cool his coffee.

"Thanks. This smells good." He opened the door and climbed down to relieve himself.

When he climbed back in the cab, there was an old, yellowed newspaper laying in his seat. He picked it up and started to place it up on the dash. There was something vaguely familiar about the old paper, and he started to ask the truck driver, "What's this?" Then he saw what it was that was familiar. A small UPI article with a dateline of Honolulu, Hawaii had a headline that read: Oahu Police Search For Suspect. Windjammer turned towards the truck driver. His eyes asked the two questions: *Who are you and are you going to bust me?*

The truck driver read the questions effortlessly, as if by osmosis. "Drink your coffee and before you think about jumping out and running, take a look at this." He handed him a current newspaper. It was the Honolulu Star Bulletin. Windjammer quickly spotted another small article with a headline and article that read:

Police Close Twenty-five Year Old Case

Honolulu Police spokesman, Ashiro Nakamine said today the homicide division is closing the twenty-five year old murder case of Richard Loeffler. Noted as one of the more notorious drug related murder cases of the seventies, Nakamine said that complete disposition of the case has been achieved.

Tory Chang admitted to the slaying of Loeffler. Chang was in his death bed in Halawa Prison where he had been incarcerated for the last eighteen years on several non-related felony convictions.

Nakamine stated that the incorrect focus of the investigation throughout had been on a Waikiki bartender who evidently fled the islands at the time of the murder. Nakamine would not divulge the name of the bartender. The Star Bulletin has confirmed from other sources the man's name was Windjammer.

Everything in Windjammer's system shut down. All he could do was stare at the article. He was oblivious to everything. The truck driver waited for him to say something, but after two or three minutes he become mildly worried. "Drink some coffee. It'll help."

"But, I don't, I don't ..." and he went back to silence. The truck driver lifted Windjammer's coffee mug to his lips and gently turned the cup into them. Eventually he could see and hear a few tentative sips of coffee go down. Then Windjammer took the cup from the truck driver and began to drink his coffee.

"I'll tell you what," the truck driver said. "Let's get on

down the road a ways, then stop for some breakfast. We can talk about it then. Give you a chance to see how those new wings feel."

"Okay," is all Windjammer could say. He was too empty to even consider what any of this meant.

A hundred miles later they were in a little western diner across the road from a small truck stop. The smell of bacon, coffee, and cigarettes was heavy. Drivers sat at the counter and filled all but one booth where they sat down. The juke box was set low, but Hank Williams was still rolling on The Lonesome Highway. A pretty young waitress took their order and went back to the kitchen laughing with several drivers about something on the way.

"Here we are," the truck driver began. "I've got a few things to tell you that will help. I know you've got questions."

"Yeah, but I don't even know how to ask them, or exactly what they are."

"That's to be expected. Think about it this way. Let's go back a ways. Let's go back to the North Shore. Back in those days you were able to tune into a force. It was not the correct force, but you were into it. Right? You could nearly become one with that force. You were so close to it you were nearly indistinguishable from it."

Windjammer had to nod in agreement.

"What if your interest, your spirit, had sought a different force? Let us even suggest that you had sought the correct force, the good force. You nevertheless would have been able to accomplish all that you did and then some. If you had sought the correct force, you would have had the ability to influence others your entire life. Look at all those people you hung with back in Hawaii. Most of them are dead today. Just think. What if you had been able to influence them with the correct force, the good force?"

He paused, and the concept began to penetrate Windjammer's fertile spiritual aura. Then he continued, "Now you've got to be careful because here is where a lot of people can falter and make a mistake. Let's say an individual has gained the awareness that knowledge of the correct force, the good force is a way to influence others. Well, you can see. This could be a good thing or a not so good thing. What if they use their knowledge to elevate themselves and simply crown themselves above the rest of us or even above the source of the correct force, the good force itself?"

The pretty waitress arrived with their breakfast and refilled their coffee. Windjammer was thinking, "Would that Christian cult leader, what was his name, Jim Jones, would he be an example of that?"

"Yes," and they both turned their attention to the scrambled eggs, biscuits, bacon, and hash browns in front of them. A minute later the truck driver said,

"What I just said is correct, but I'm not sure it really paints the picture that will help you come to terms with all that's gone on."

"Keep going. I'm with you so far."

"Last night, you remember the strange CB voice that you said to yourself, 'This guy thinks he is an angel and is here to warn us about the judgment.' You remember?"

"How could I forget? The guy sounded like he'd wiped out on too many thirty footers."

"Maybe he did. Maybe he didn't. Maybe he's an angel. Maybe he isn't. That's not terribly important. There were two things he said that were important. In fact they are key to helping you get a handle on all that's going on, and one other thing I will add myself. You ready?"

"Shoot." Evidently Windjammer's new wings also came with a new set of ears.

"He said, 'With God all things are possible.' He said that Jesus said 'He who has ears to hear, let him hear.' And now the point I add, and actually the maybe or maybe not fallen angel alluded to it also. The focus of those who possess the spirit, the knowledge of the correct force, the good force, should be on that force, on God, on their service to him, not on themselves. That was Jim Jones's error. If you can grasp this you will come to see how the miracle of those two newspapers this morning could be. You will come to understand why I am here with you now. You will come to understand why your last twenty-five years of running from a crime you didn't commit doesn't have to be in vain."

The truck driver paused, and added, "And you will understand a lot more than that. It will come immediately in some ways and slowly in other ways. The understanding sinks in on different people in different ways. But the key to any person's ability to receive this understanding is the acceptance of the sacrifice of the Son of God, Jesus the Christ, Jesus the Lamb. You now have a choice. You have now heard the truth with your new ears. You won't need a guide or a helper in this earthly dimension to lead you to the correct choice I hope you will make. The Great Spirit, the one true spirit, the Holy Spirit is there for that purpose. You will know when, and how, and why to make your choice."

* * *

They were outside the diner. The sun was dancing off the mountains all around. Men in cowboy hats, faded work shirts, and boots were coming and going. The truck driver and Windjammer walked across the road and climbed up into the big truck. The truck driver fired the big diesel up, and they rolled off towards Flagstaff. Seventy-seven miles down the road the truck driver pulled over on the dusty shoulder, the sun higher in the sky now, the day warming up. An intersection lay a few feet ahead.

"I'll be turning off here for Flagstaff. You're welcome to come along with me if you like."

"Thanks, but I think I'll keep heading west."

"You still going to California?"

"No, I think I'll try to go on to Hawaii."

"Good luck. I'll be seeing you."

Windjammer looked into those deep hazel eyes. Their eyes held each other for a moment, and Windjammer said, "Yep, I'll be seeing you too, truck driver."

They shook hands; Windjammer grabbed his bag and climbed down.

The big truck eased away slowly, and a bolt of realization came over Windjammer as the truck began picking up speed. *I don't even know his name!*

He started to run after him, but realized it was too late. Then he noticed for the first time the truck driver had his name painted neatly and in small letters on the door – JABEZ.

As the big truck gained momentum and speed, Windjammer watched it get farther and farther away. He lifted his arm up high and waved fare-the-well. The truck was nearly out of sight, but its response was heard perfectly by Windjammer – seven loud and powerful toots from the air horn. Windjammer had the ears to hear.

* * *

Toby stared at that paragraph. Then he quickly turned to the copyright page to check the copyright date. It was copyrighted in 2000.

Then he turned to read the credits and marketing blurbs from other writers. Several different writers wrote that the author is gaining a reputation for his novels actually being works of nonfiction. They said quite a stir is being drummed up by editors who say they have reason to believe the author's stories are in fact the true to life events of some mysterious real-life truck driver. The publisher even suggested that readers check out the web site for more information.

Toby did so and was amazed when he read an article stating that the writer's pen name is just that – a pen name. As far as anyone can tell, the actual identity of the writer is unknown.

Toby laughed out loud. "I know who it is."

If you enjoyed this book the author invites you to visit his website at www.garyhbaker.com. where you can read an excerpt of his second book West Bound, Hammer Down, Trouble in Montana which is due out in the fall of 2008

Gary welcomes your comments about Rookie Truck Driver. He also encourages truck drivers to submit their best stories so they may find their way into future books in this series.

1547926

Made in the USA